COMMENTARY UPON
THE MAYA-TZENTAL PEREZ CODEX

COMMENTARY UPON THE MAYA-TZENTAL PEREZ CODEX

WILLIAM E. GATES

ISBN: 978-93-5614-385-2

Published: 1910

LECTOR HOUSE LLP
E-MAIL: lectorpublishing@gmail.com

PAPERS OF
THE PEABODY MUSEUM OF AMERICAN ARCHAEOLOGY
AND ETHNOLOGY, HARVARD UNIVERSITY
VOL. VI.—NO. 1

COMMENTARY UPON
THE MAYA-TZENTAL PEREZ CODEX

WITH A CONCLUDING NOTE UPON
THE LINGUISTIC PROBLEM OF
THE MAYA GLYPHS

BY

WILLIAM E. GATES

PROFESSOR IN SCHOOL OF ANTIQUITY, INTERNATIONAL
THEOSOPHICAL HEADQUARTERS, POINT LOMA, CALIFORNIA

1910

NOTE

IN presenting this Commentary on the Codex Perez to students of American Archaeology, the Peabody Museum adds another paper to its series relating to the study of the hieroglyphic writing of the ancient peoples of Mexico and Central America.

The Museum is fortunate in adding to its collaborators Mr. William E. Gates, of Point Loma, California, who for more than ten years has been an earnest student of American hieroglyphs. From his lifelong studies in linguistics in connection with his research in "the motifs of civilizations and cultures," he comes well-equipped to take up the difficult and all-absorbing study of American hieroglyphic writing. Mr. Gates has materially advanced this study by his reproduction of the glyphs in type. These type-forms he has used first in his reproduction of the Codex Perez, and now in this Commentary they are used for the first time in printing. The method used in the construction of this font of type is explained by Mr. Gates in the following pages. This important aid to the study will be highly appreciated by all students of American hieroglyphs, as it will greatly facilitate the presentation of the results of future research.

It will be seen that this Commentary is more in the line of suggestion to be expanded after further studies, than in the way of conclusions.

At the close of the paper the author presents the general deductions he has drawn from his comparative study of languages and cultures. His concluding paragraph forcibly presents the hope that the understanding of the Maya glyphs will furnish new and important data in the life history of man.

F. W. PUTNAM

PEABODY MUSEUM
October, 1910

PEREZ CODEX: PAGE 6.

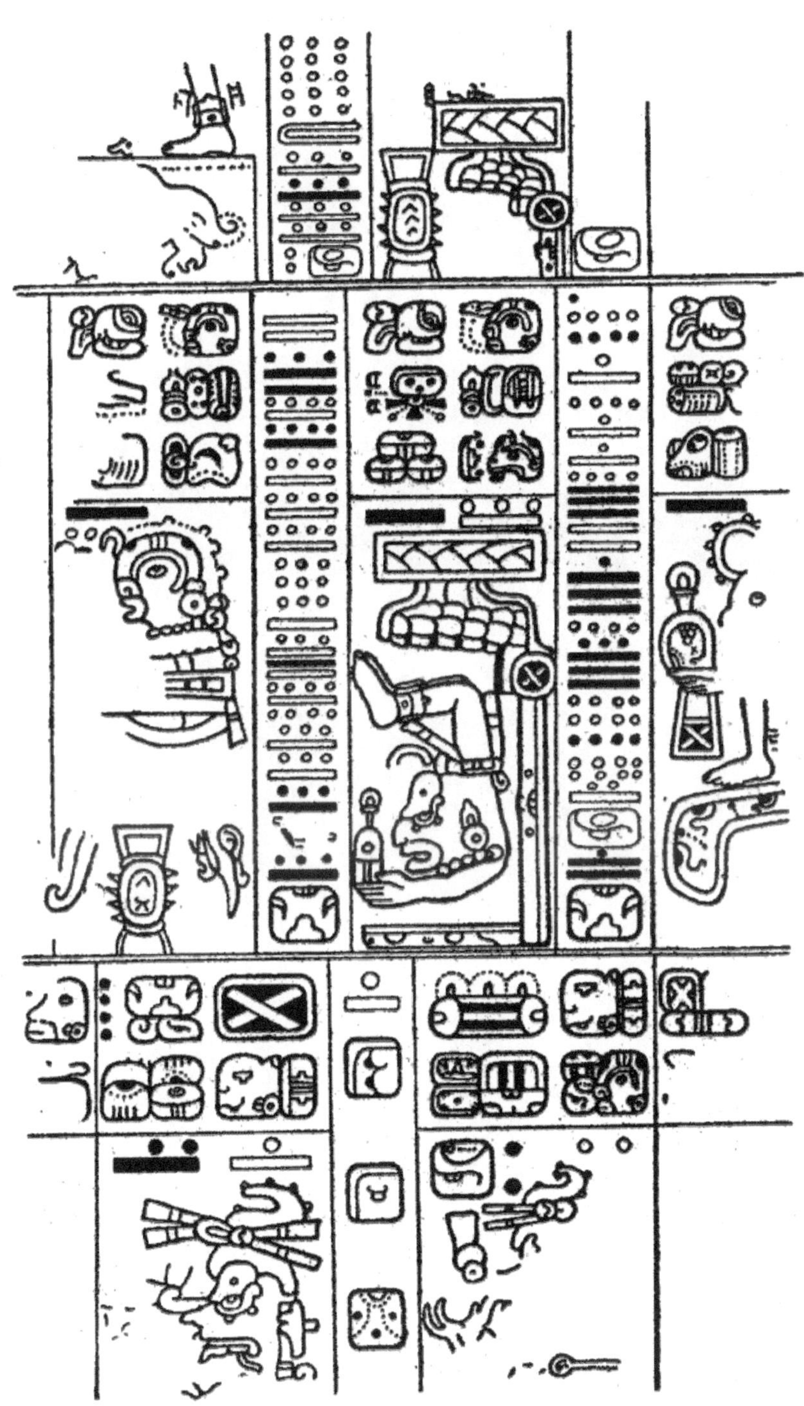

PEREZ CODEX: PAGE 17.

CONTENTS

THE PEREZ CODEX

THE PEREZ CODEX was discovered just fifty years ago by Prof. Léon de Rosny, while searching through the Bibliothèque Impériale, Paris, in the hope of bringing to light some documents of interest for the then newly awakened study of Pre-Columbian America. It was found by him in a basket among a lot of old papers, black with dust and practically abandoned in a chimney corner. From a few words with the name Perez, written on a torn scrap of paper then around it but since lost, it received its name.

Being restored to its proper place in the Library, it was in 1864 photographed by order of M. Victor Duruy, Minister of Instruction, and a few copies issued without further explanatory notes than the printed wrappers. The number of copies is stated by Prof. de Rosny to have been very small; in Leclerc's *Bibl. Amér.* (1878, No. 2290) it is given as only 10, and in Brasseur's *Bibl. Mex.-Guat.* (page 95), as 50. A copy is in the library of the Bureau of Ethnology at Washington, and referred to in their publications as a most fortunate acquisition. I had the good fortune to secure a copy some ten years ago, and one other has recently appeared in a Leipzig catalog at a high price. Beyond these I have not traced any other copy.

In 1872 Prof. de Rosny published a reproduction, drawn by hand, which, as stated by him later, may be disregarded for practical purposes.[1]

In 1887 he issued a facsimile edition in colors, 85 copies, which up to the present time has remained the only attempt to show the Codex in its proper colors, and has become exceedingly difficult to procure; so much so that it was only after seven years search that I was able to secure my own copy.[2]

In 1888 he reissued the Codex, uncolored, with the same letter-press, and in an edition of 100 copies. This has also become scarce.

Each of these three editions has its advantages and disadvantages. The colored edition of 1887, having been worked over by hand, in lithography, is defective in various places, both as regards the black of the figures and glyphs, and in the colors. Coloring exists on the original codex which was not reproduced at all in the edition, and the colors given are in many cases not exact. Thus on pages 19 and 20 two different reds are used for the backgrounds, whereas but one is found in the original; on pages 15, 16 the figures are a turquoise green, and on pages 17, 18 an olive green, the correct color for all four being turquoise green.

I have been able to find no inaccuracy in the 1888 edition, which is indeed

[1] In *Archives paléographiques de l'Orient et de l'Amérique*, atlas, t. I, pl. 117-142.

[2] In his *Commentar zur Pariser Mayahandschrift*, Danzig, 1903, Dr. Förstemann does not know of the existence of this edition.

stated in the introduction to be entirely by mechanical process, without hand intervention; but being reproduced by printer's ink in black only, not only do the colors not appear, but the chromatic values are actually far inferior to the photographs of 1864. It was stated further by Prof. de Rosny that some features of the MS. had been lost by deterioration in the 25 years previous to his editions of 1887 and 1888, but this I have not been able to verify in any important point.

The photographs and the edition of 1888 are to all general purposes identical; but, notwithstanding that the photographs are steadily yellowing by age, the chromatic values are so far superior that I have continually come to find them the court of final decision in doubtful matters. In a very considerable number of instances a close examination of the photographs has suggested the presence of faint lines of color on glyphs or figures, which was entirely indistinguishable in both of the printed editions, and which was yet in every case confirmed, although sometimes with difficulty, by the examination of the original MS.

The proved value, as well as the scarcity, of these photographs was so great, that in 1905 I had my set photographed twice, by dry and wet plate processes, and a few copies printed after a careful comparison and selection of the two sets of plates. It is from these that the present edition has grown.[3]

The present edition, save for the photographs thus reproduced, having been entirely redrawn, and partly restored, it is fitting to detail just what has been done in this respect.

At the very beginning of my introduction to Maya studies the enormous burdens placed on research therein at every turn, bore upon me as upon every other student. The subject and its possibilities stimulate enthusiasm to the highest degree; the rewards of success are greater than those of any like problem today; and yet, fifty years since the present Codex was discovered, and thirty years since Dr. Förstemann's unsurpassable edition of the Dresden Codex, the actual workers on the problem are the barest handful. A few scattered and obscure references amongst the volumes on volumes of Spanish writers, nearly all untranslated, most of them scarce or almost unprocurable, and many not even printed, make up the literature to be searched out. And a few points of decipherment won and safely fixed by the researchers, from Brasseur, de Rosny, Pousse, Brinton and others a generation ago, to Messrs. Bowditch, Seler, Goodman and a few others of today, are all we have — standing out in a wilderness of guesses by many writers, needless of naming.

Of course the prime and absolute necessity of such a study is true facsimiles; but the task of using even these, taken as they must be from much defaced inscriptions and manuscripts, is too obvious for comment. So from the very first

---

[3] *Codex Perez*: Maya-Tzental. Redrawn and Slightly Restored, and with the Coloring as it originally stood, so far as possible, given on the basis of a new and minute examination of the Codex itself. Mounted in the form of the Original. Accompanied by a Reproduction of the 1864 Photographs; also by the entire Text of the Glyphs, unemended but with some restorations, Printed from Type, and arranged in Parallel Columns for convenience of study and comparison. Drawn and edited by William E. Gates. (*Privately printed.*) Point Loma, 1909.

of my studies I began to cherish thoughts of the day when Maya could be printed with type, and classified indexes to the glyphs at hand. From one point of view such facilities can only be expected to come *after* decipherment; from another, in absence of bilingual keys, they are a necessity *before* that can be attained. So far as his work covers, a great deal has been done in this line by Mr. A. P. Maudslay in the field of the inscriptions.

At the very outset therefore I must enter acknowledgment of the assistance that I owe to the courtesy at that time of Prof. F. W. Putnam, of Peabody Museum, and Mr. Chas. P. Bowditch, in placing, with a freedom by no means universal among curators and researchers, their material at my disposal, with privilege of copying. I am safe to say that while I have reclassified the glyphs for my own use as my studies went on, yet without the copy which by Mr. Bowditch's courtesy I was allowed to make of his card index to the glyphs of the three codices, as a start, this edition of the Perez Codex would not yet have reached daylight through the many other occupations among which Maya studies have had to take their chances.

At first it seemed possible to prepare a font of separate types for the various elements of the compound glyphs we find in the texts; but after having such a font made a number of years ago, and printing a couple of pages of the Dresden Codex, the result was unsatisfactory; it became evident that the proper Maya font of type must be both separate and composite, as is used in Chinese, and not separate only as we have for Egyptian. The type for the text cards of this edition have therefore been made this way.

As to the colored plates of the Codex herewith, it is evident that nothing whatever is gained by preserving the irregularities of the defaced parts of the Codex, while everything is to be gained by making all as clear and distinct as possible. The first step therefore was to have a set of photographed enlargements of two diameters, made direct from the 1864 issue. From these I made careful tracings, myself, of the black figure and glyph lines of the original, making at the same time the separate enlarged drawings from which the type were afterwards made. At this first drawing only the evident, the indisputable parts were drawn. The type forms were then classified, arranged in parallel columns, and compared. All was then gone over, and new points settled on the basis of the familiarity thus gained. It is a fair estimate to say that this process of checking and verifying was gone through, first to last, down to the final proof-reading of the printed sheets, some fifty times.

One most important fact was established by this process, and must be noted. In the Perez Codex at least, *nothing is to be taken for granted*, nothing charged to a careless scribe, and no variants regarded as being identical in value—with a very few exceptions, to which I shall advert later. Wherever there remains enough of any glyph to show its characteristic strokes, it can be regarded as safely indicated; whenever the strokes are not just those characteristic of any glyph, it cannot be inferred. Down to the very end of the various revisions I found myself able to add glyphs which at first seemed hopeless, and yet when once seen became clear and plain. Relying on the presence of the photographs to check the work, I have thus added a very considerable number to the glyphs at first apparent. In some cases, as in 6-b-11 and 17, and especially in 8-b-7, 8, 10, where glyphs were only partially erased, but no other instances of perfect glyphs existed to compare them with, I have let them alone, without attempting restoration. In short, I may have made some errors of eye, but I have guessed nothing.

In a very few places I have restored glyphs totally erased, relying on the parallelism of the passages. Such are some of the Ahau-numbers in the upper sections of pages 2 to 11, and in the central sections on those pages, the initial pairs of glyphs on pages 15 to 18-a, b, c, the first columns of pages 19 and 20, and a few day-signs on pages 21, 23 and 24. These glyphs are all necessitated by their different series, and hence can cause no confusions; while it seemed advantageous to have them before the eye. A fair instance of the procedure is shown on page 3-b-1, 3. The temptation was strong to put the usual 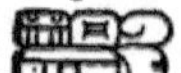 glyph here as on all the other pages, but the slight variation in the lines left  of glyph 3-b-3 forbade it.

The restoration will further be found a little bolder on the type-cards than in the colored plates, where I have in general only endeavored to reproduce what could be seen actually present. The glyphs restored on the upper part of page 7 would seem hopeless at first sight; but they are well-known and common forms, and the characteristic traces shown on the photographs belong to these and to no others known.

The cards of type-printed text, in parallel columns for convenience of study, are self-explanatory. Such an arrangement has from the first seemed to me indispensable for proper study and comparison. The paging of the de Rosny editions I have retained, except to change the practically blank page 1 to be page 25, since to number this as 1 is confusing. For the divisions and the numbering of the glyphs I have made my own arrangement. It is possible that section *b* on pages 2 to 11 should only go to the bottom line of the central figure, leaving section *d* to read clear across the page, and another section to be made to the left of the nearly erased figures at the bottom; but the chances as shown by the lining and arrangement of the columns seemed to favor it as I have given it. Only final decipherment can decide definitely.

THE COLORS

The colors of the Codex afforded a number of questions for solution, some of which I have cleared up and embodied in the plates; a few are I believe insoluble. I have also been able to add a few wholly new points, not indicated by any of the preceding editions.

Being unable to make a personal examination of the original, I prepared from my enlarged black drawings, above mentioned, another full set including the figures and all glyphs or other parts showing any suggestions of color. Upon these I prepared a list of nearly 200 questions covering every detail, together with certain general specifications, and had the whole made the subject of a careful and exhaustive comparison with the original at the Bibliothèque Nationale. This report, when duly returned with the various details set out, with the various colors shown in their exact tints by water-colors, and with a special analysis of the question of the fading of the colors, was again checked and verified by the evidence of the three editions.

In doubtful questions arising from faded colors, I have sought to show the condition of the original as it exists today. In the solid red backgrounds and other places I have aimed to show as far as possible what the Codex looked like when fresh.

This question as to what all the colors in detail were when fresh, I do not feel that I have quite solved. The following palette scheme seems to me about as near as the data permit us to formulate.

A permanent black, being the parts reproduced in black in the present edition.

A brick-red, tinged with crimson, used for backgrounds, red numerals, and probably elsewhere. This we may call unfading red.

A genuine brown, as on the animals, pages 5-a, 8-a; perhaps also elsewhere as lining ornament.

A pale pink as flesh color on the human figures.

A blue, as on the possible katun number series on pages 23 and 24.

A turquoise-green, with varying amounts of blue tinge, on the spotted figures and in the numeral columns of pages 15 to 18; also, with somewhat less of the blue, for the "water" bands on pages 21 to 24.

The above colors are all definite and positive.

Then next appears a brownish color used for lining or ornamenting various glyphs, and the clothing, headdress, etc., etc., of the figures. We find many shades from a pale neutral up to a darker clear brown, and also a definitely reddish, as on the tail of the bird on the right side of page 23. This brown may be a fading of the red of the backgrounds and numerals, but the permanence of the color in these latter places is so positive that I believe it is not so. I think it should be regarded as separate.

We next come to a color question related directly to decipherment, that of the very difficult numeral columns on pages 15 to 18. There is no practical reason discernable for the use of alternating colors save the avoidance of confusion between bar combinations. Three bars together of different colors stand of course for three 5's; of one color they would make a single number 15. We therefore find here our above black, red and blue-green alternating and clearly marked in places; but we also find many numerals of varying shades of brownish, bistre and grayish. I called for especial care in the examination of these points on the original Codex, and the water-color sheets and explanatory notes show in detail the facts of the present state of the Codex. Prior to the examination I supposed that these faded numerals were a faded red, but this is stated in the report to be certainly not the case; the suggestion is made that they are probably faded blacks.

From the latter conclusion I am inclined in part to dissent, at least as to certain passages, for two reasons. These are, first the actual permanence of the above noted main colors, everywhere else; and second, passages in the second columns of pages 16 and 17. In each of these we find faded brown or gray bars, so placed between or next to plain black bars as would give, were they faded blacks, more than three black bars together.

Another point on page 17 is to be noted. In the top section, first column, are five blue 3's. Some of these blue dots, as shown in the 1887 edition and in my water-colors, have faded to the same light brown seen elsewhere. The brown and the blue 5 in the second column of this page, middle division, as just mentioned, have also an identical chromatic value in the photographs.

My whole conclusion therefore, so far as I can formulate one, is that in these columns we have:

Red, black, and blue-green numerals, as shown. Some of the blue numerals seem to have been *outlined* with black, of which traces still appear on the original, are seen in the photographs, and indicated in the present color plates.

Several instances where the Codex has been rubbed so as to leave only the outlines of original black numerals. These are now gray in the original, and I have left them as black outlines, touched in with gray.

Finally, a number of pale brown numerals which are either faded blue-greens, or else indicate a fourth color in the original. Which of these alternatives is the true one, I cannot say.

The original Codex is still in practically as good condition as when the three editions were taken from it. The material of which it is made is a maguey paper of grayish tinge, and not a yellowish brown as would be inferred from the 1887 edition. This is noteworthy, as the wearing away of the coating with which the paper was surfaced for the writing, does not leave a brownish place which, as in the 1887 edition, might be mistaken for traces of applied color. This coating is indeed better preserved in places than is shown by the 1887 edition; thus the headdress at the extreme left of page 20, just to the right of the restored 8 Ezanab on the present color plates, is shown with the coating all erased and the black writing as if left on the ground-paper—which is incorrect.

THE PAGES IN DETAIL

Coming then to the question of the subject-matter of the Codex, I feel that little is in order beyond a simple analytical description of the different pages, rather than any attempt at an interpretation. The road of general deductions from superficial resemblances between unknown elements and the details of other known things from other times and places, is strewn by the wrecks of too many theories to be attractive traveling. I am firmly convinced of the greatness and importance of the study we have before us, and the exalted civilization which produced it; but I do not know how to interpret these monuments. Indeed the very persistence with which the interpretation (which will certainly be self-evident and everywhere applicable when it does finally come) still eludes us, is a sufficient proof that we have not yet found the right road. When we do, great doorways to the past of mankind will open of themselves, and we will know more of human life and evolution than we now guess. Until then we can only describe, classify, and try to get rid of some of the mechanical impedimenta of the search.

What we have of the Perez Codex is manifestly but a fragment; the extent of it originally we have no means of even guessing. It is fortunate however that what we have gives several practically complete chapters or portions of the work. Taking first the side of the MS. paged 2 to 12, we find the entire side covered by a series of pictures with text, all identical in arrangement. The few remaining traces on page 12 show its likeness to the others, for we see in their proper places parts of the Tun-glyph on which the figures on the upper section are seated; of the Cimi, Tun and Cauac glyphs just as in pages 11-c-2, 6 and 8; also of the columns of glyphs to the left, and traces of the headdress. As will appear further, at least two more pages are required to complete this series, and it is as good a supposition as any other that they were those which would be numbered 1 and 13—that is, one before page 2 and one after page 12. For convenience of reference the divisions of these pages may be lettered from *a* to *e*; *a* being given to the upper portion, *b* to the left columns of glyphs, *e* to the large middle picture, and *c* and *d* to the text divisions above and below this.

Taking up first the central figures, section *e*, we find in each a standing figure, with ceremonial headdress of varying character, offering a dragon's head (a universal symbol of wisdom) to another figure, seated on a cushioned dais, the side of which bears various "constellation" signs. The latter in turn extends his hands, either holding some object, or else in a simple gesture. The standing figures are all almost completely preserved; the seated ones unfortunately largely or wholly obliterated. In front of the standing ministrant is a vase of offerings, usually a triple Kan figure, and in two cases with knives. In the upper part of the picture, facing in every case but one towards the ministrant, is a bird figure, different on each page, and having in two cases a human head. On each page is an Ahau sign with red numeral, all of them together forming a series which (starting on the supposed page 1 with 4 Ahau) gives the succession 4, 2, 13, 11, 9, 7, 5, 3, 1, 12, 10, 8, 6; in other words the numbers of thirteen consecutive katuns. The Ahau numerals 13, 11, 9, on pages 3, 4 and 5, are entirely distinct, and enough traces appear on other pages to establish this as a katun series beyond question. If this chapter includes just a round of numbers it would of course be complete in 13 pages. The chapter may be historical in contents, but the presence of this numeral Ahau-series clearly relates these pages to successive katuns in some way, whatever other bearings they may have. The ten pages thus in some way definitely have to do with the lapse of 72,000 days, or not quite 200 solar years, and the extension of the series to a full cycle of 20 katuns is quite likely. The background of this section *e* is red on each alternate page.

Returning now to section *a*, we find on each page three figures, nearly all of persons or animals, seated on a large base practically identical with the tun-glyph. Fourteen of the backgrounds to these figures are red. Above each figure there seems to have been at least six glyphs, of which but very few are left. Above these is a space entirely erased. In the center of the section on each page is a column containing at least two Ahaus with red numerals. The numerals of the upper row exceed those of the lower by 6; each row decreases from page to page by 4. The erased margins of the MS. do not afford space for another picture besides the three, on either side, but they do just give room for another Ahau-column on the left of each page. If this second Ahau-column existed, we have again the katun-series repeated in each row across. If it did not exist, the series (reading from the supposed page 1) of 13, 9, 5, etc., and 7, 3, 12, etc., decreasing by 4's, give the numbers of successive tuns. Once again the question of whether a simple number-round of thirteen terms, or a full round of twenty terms, whether tuns or katuns, was originally displayed on the Codex, must be left undetermined. It is further to be noted that faint but exact traces of a third Ahau, on a higher line, appear on page 5, as well as some doubtful traces on page 8. No definite relationship between the pictures of this section *a* and those of section *e* is apparent.

Section *b* is made up of 45 or more glyphs in three columns. The first column is almost totally erased on every page, and I have disregarded it both in assigning reference numbers and in the type cards. The other two columns I have numbered in double column sequence downwards; but this can be regarded as solely for convenience' sake. The glyph which is three times repeated at the beginning of page 2, and recurs in parallel position repeated two to five times on each page, is the most common glyph in the whole Codex. It is identifiable probably 38 times, including twice at the top of the erased *first* column on page 4. It heads the second column several times on every page, except 7, which is too erased for any determination, and page 3, where a slight variation in what is left of the postfix at b-3 forbade its insertion under the rules I have given limiting restorations. I suspect that this glyph should be repeated at 3-b-9 and 11-b-9, for the following reason. In positions b-6, b-8 or b-10 of each page occurs a certain face-glyph  that is found nowhere else in either the Perez, Dresden or Tro.-Cort. codices. If the initial glyph is repeated at 3-b-9 and 11-b-9 as suggested, then (with a slight variation on page 4) this series of repetitions of the initial glyph will in each case be closed by the face-glyph in question.

A marked feature of section *b* is the occurrence, near the bottom of each page, of a Cauac-sign, with or without the wing-postfix, and with prefixed and superfixed numerals, exactly as is so common in connexion with the C h u e n - sign on the Inscriptions. This Cauac-sign is usually accompanied by an Ahau and a Tun, each with numerals that are for the most part erased. This combination suggests distance-numbers and dates, somewhat as on the Inscriptions; in this case the double-numbered Cauacs would stand for so many uinals plus so many days. The following combinations, besides the one above, are also found:

Section *c* consists of 16 glyphs in two rows, above the central picture. Glyphs 15 and 16 on each page are erased. The chief general characteristic is the frequent repetition of the Cimi-compound, ; the repetition on each page of a Cauac-sign with single or double numerals as in section *b*; and of Tun-compounds, with subfix and with varying prefixes (frequently faces), as especially see page 5.

Section *d* is a triple row of glyphs, originally 21 in some instances, but with many now erased. I am able to establish few general characteristics for this section, save again the frequency of the Cimi-compound as in section *c*, of various Tun-compounds, and of the two glyphs and With the exception of 10-b-4, the face with the tau-eye occurs only in this section *d* and on pages 15 to 18. This glyph is exceedingly common both in Dres. and Tro.-Cort, the form in which it appears at 3-d-4, 6, occurring (including its secondary compounds) no less than 126 times in Dres. and 33 times in Tro.-Cort.

Beneath section *d* are the remains of red numerals and of heads and headdresses of figures which are now too much erased to give any basis for comment.

A most marked feature of the Codex is the very large number of Tun-compounds, a feature confined exclusively, with one exception, to the present pages 2 to 11, and pages 23, 24. A classified list shows 28 compounds of this glyph,  20 of these showing the subfix, and combined with a face or other prefix. The connexion of this fact with the Tun-bases of section *a*, and with the katun-rounds shown by the Ahau-series above referred to, is manifest.

To sum up the general characteristics of this side of the MS., and without attempting to interpret any separate glyphs, we find the following data:

The Cimi-compound  and its sub-compound  occurs 25 times.

The numeral-compounded Cauac occurs 20 times.

The glyph  occurs 13 times on this side and once on page 23.

The Chuen-compound  occurs 19 times and probably oftener—once only on the other side of the MS.

The various Tun-glyphs occur 45 times, on the two sides.

The face-glyph  occurs 10 times.

The Kan-Ymix glyph  occurs 10 times.

The glyph  occurs 37 times on this side and, with a prefix and a changed postfix, once on page 24.

With the exceptions noted, none of the above glyphs occur at all on the reverse side of the MS.

There are finally 19 different Yax () compounds, occurring in all 25 times, 16 of them on this side of the MS.

With three exceptions the above glyphs are the only ones that are repeated in the Codex with any marked frequency. The three exceptions are the face with tau-eye, already  mentioned, and the two glyphs occurring as an initial  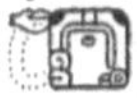 pair twelve times on pages 15 to 18, sections *a*, *b*, *c*.

Of month signs used as such I am only   satisfied of 12 Cumhu, at 18-b-4 and of 16 Zac, at 4-c-7. The glyph  at 7-c-2 may also be 1 Yaxkin.

The only cardinal point sign is that of the West,  occurring at 4-b-14 and again at 16-a-6.

There are besides these numeral Cauacs, 15 other Cauac  compounds, occurring in all 17 times on this side, and twice on pages 23, 24.

Upon turning over the Codex, we find that whereas on the side we have been considering the scribe limited himself to the conventional red numerals and backgrounds, with here and there a touch of brown, upon this other side we have a wealth of color united with a harmony of composition and structure that marks a very high degree of artistic skill. It is not alone the accuracy of the drawing and the writing, such as we have noted in connexion with the study of the glyphs, but the whole manuscript as it lies open before us shows that sense of proportion, that ability to unify without seeming effort a multitude of details into a perfectly balanced whole, which is the positive mark of developed and genuine culture. When we remember the exceeding difficulty of combining primary colors into a brilliancy that is not garish, and the equal difficulty of achieving artistic mastery in a conventional treatment of forms, we are simply forced to recognize that we have here the evidence of an advanced school of art with full rights of independent citizenship. If the figures look strange and sometimes distorted, we must remember that our whole training has been in the realistic school, by which we are prone to judge all others, but by which they must not be judged. We have no more right to weigh these compositions in the scales of our art motifs than we have to weigh Greek rhythm of quantity or Saxon of alliteration against our weights by which we measure rhythm of rhyme and stress. In fact it is impossible for us even to judge concerning the true harmonic effect of these other measures, and it may well be doubted whether the very soul itself of our meter is not empty and tinny as compared with these others—quality for quality.

There is one great broad line that divides the nations and civilizations of the earth, past and present, in all their arts of expression. We may call it that of the ideographic as against the literal. It controls the inner form of language and of languages; it manifests in the passage of thought from man to man; it determines whether the writing of the people shall be hieroglyphic or alphabetic; it gives both life and form to the ideals of their art. It is a distinction that was clearly recognized by Wilhelm von Humboldt, when he laid down that the incorporative characteristic essential to all the American languages is the result of the exaltation of the imaginative over the ratiocinative elements of mind.

The time has passed when we think that the absence of our perspective drawing in Japanese pictures is due to the fact that these "children of nature" never happened to recognize that a thing looks smaller in proportion to its distance, so that they ought to come to us to learn. We have come, in some measure if not yet fully, to recognize that whereas we show a thing to the eye, these other peoples suggest a thought to the mind, by their pictures. And we should remember, and remember always, that while our modern art having won its technical and artistic skill within the past few hundred years, is now beginning to emancipate itself from the materialism of the eye by efforts towards the "impressionist" methods, these ancient peoples had long since arrived at the ability to convey "impressions" through the medium of harmonious compositions of the most rigid conventional elements—an artistic achievement which those who know its difficulties can alone begin to appreciate.

It may be quite easily forgiven to one trained with Western, modern eyes, who at first sight of these monuments, in total ignorance of their meanings, sees them as strange or grotesque. But when, as their strangeness wears away, one comes to see the unfailing accuracy with which the glyphs are drawn, one's opinion of their makers has to change. And when, with this familiarity gained, one advances to an appreciation of the work in its bearings as a whole, one has to acknowledge himself facing the production of craftsmen who had the inheritance of not only generations, but ages of training. Such a combination of complete mastery in composition, perfect control of definite and fixed forms, and hand technique, can grow up from barbarism in no few hundred years. I would hesitate to think it could even come in a few thousands, unless they were years of greater settledness and peaceful civilization than our two thousand years of disturbed and warring European Christendom have yet had an example of to show us. It is easy enough in the absence of definite historical records, and in our general ignorance of human evolution, to theorize and speculate about it all; but the commonly accepted picture in our minds of a few savage wandering tribes settling and growing up in this country some several hundred or a thousand years after the Christian era, simply will not fit in with the fact of their ability to produce such works a few hundred years later. Had we nothing but the Perez Codex and Stela P at Copan, the merits of their execution alone, weighed simply in comparison with observed history elsewhere, would prove that we have to do not with the traces of an ephemeral, but with the remains of a wide-spread, settled race and civilization, worthy to be ranked with or beyond even such as the Roman, in its endurance, development and influence in the world, and the beginnings of whose culture are still totally unknown. As to the Codex before us, we can only imagine what the beauty, especially of the pages we now come to discuss, must have been when the whole was fresh and perfect.

The second side of the Codex has to be treated in four divisions or chapters, the first of which includes pages 15 to 18. For numerical reasons which will appear, this chapter must probably have begun, however, at least one page further to the left.

These four pages are laid out with three main divisions, upper, middle and lower. Too much of the upper section is erased for any comment other than that its arrangement seems to have been parallel in all respects with the middle section. This latter shows three subsections, the backgrounds in some cases being red,[4] containing each a picture (probably of a god or a human figure in every instance), surmounted by a black and a red numeral and by six glyphs, in double column. This gives 12 subsections for the four pages, which we may refer to respectively as 15-*a*, *b*, *c*, etc. Of the initial pairs of glyphs in each subsection many are complete, and no section is left without the correct traces of the corresponding glyph for one or other of the positions; so that although 5 of the 24 glyphs are totally erased, we may safely restore them all. Other features of the comparative use and frequency of the glyphs on these pages have already been given.

At the top of each picture is found a black and a red numeral. These form the consecutive black "counters" or interval numbers, and the corresponding red day numbers of subdivided tonalamatls, so common in Dres. and Tro.-Cort. It is customary to find these tonalamatls divided into fifths or fourths, 52 or 65 days respectively—four or five trecenas. At the 53rd or 66th day the initial red number is again reached, and the calculation is (by hypothesis) repeated, starting again at the left with a new day-sign below the first. Such a column is seen in the lower part of

---

[4] Dr. Förstemann (*Comm. z. Par. Mayahds.*) speaks of the background to the central figure on page 16 as black, instead of red; he also describes the number columns as made up of red and black numerals only. There are many similar errors in his Commentary, due to his ignorance of the colors, and to the obscurity of the photographic reproductions.

page 17, where we find 6 Oc, Ik, Ix; these are to be completed by restoring below an erased Cimi and Ezanab, completing the 260 days and bringing us around again to 6 Oc. The total of all the black "counters" in any series must always be some multiple of 13, usually 52 or 65, as stated. And since each "counter" is the interval between its adjoining red numbers, wherever a red and a black number are given, the other red number, whether before or after, can always be filled in.

No traces of this initial column appear for the series in the middle division, and several of the numerals are also erased. Two obscurities must be cleared up before trying to fill out the series. On page 16 right is a partly erased black numeral, which from the traces may be either 10 or 11. Taking it as 10, we have 13 plus 10 equals an erased red 10; plus 5 (on page 17) equals the red 2 below the 5. This verifies so far. But we next find—plus 5 equals 8, which is of course incorrect. An inspection of the MS. and the photographs reveals a reddish spot (or perhaps even *three* such spots) in the extreme upper right corner of the picture space, 17-a, and also a dark spot *under* the black 5 in 17-b. It is possible that the separated red dots (one doubtful) are to be read together as 3; or that the red dots under the 5 are to be disregarded in the count (just as is the red 8 on the next page, 18-a), and the red number for 17-a found in the upper right, above the seated figure. If the red number in 17-a is 3, the two numbers in 16-c must be 11. Or it may be assumed that the spot under the 5 in 17-b belongs to it, making 6 instead of 5, which figures out. The final result is the same, as we have either 10 and 6, or 11 and 5, in these two places, and either reaches properly the clear red 8 in 17-b.

In 18-a we find black 26, with a small red 8 below, and a large red 13 in the usual place at the side. The red 8 will have to be disregarded, as not part of the series, which requires 13, and nothing else.

We may now possibly set down the series as follows, using small figures above the line for the black counters, and putting in parentheses all numbers restored:

$$(6)^3 9^{(6)} (2)^5 7^6 13^{11} (11)^5 3^5 8^5 (13)^{26} 13^{10} 10, \text{ or else}$$
$$(6)^3 9^{(6)} (2)^5 7^6 13^{10} (10)^5 2^6 8^5 (13)^{26} 13^{10} 10$$

This leaves us the black number at the beginning, in 15-a, and both numbers at the end, 18-c, still not filled in. Adding together all the counters we get 82, plus at least the two missing black numbers, one at each end. If the total were 104, we might expect it to have been comprised within the four subsections 15-a to 18-a. But 104 is not a tonalamatl fraction. 130 days, although a tonalamatl half, is an unknown division, and would hardly get into the space. If we begin the series in the upper division of the page (as occurs in Dres.) and come around to the middle division, the probabilities would require that it displayed a full series of 260 days, and again also that it began *to the left* of page 15. The probabilities of this series as it is, therefore, indicate at least a page 14 to the left, arranged like the other four, and forming one chapter with them.

We have now to deal with the puzzling numeral columns, in alternating colors, found to the left of each subsection of the upper and middle divisions—24 columns in all. These have been referred to at some length in the preliminary discussion of the colors, and there is little more that can be said. As there said, the entire reason for alternating the colors can not be certainly assumed. Alternation of color occurs not only where it is needed to distinguish bars, but also where we have only lines of dots, which are of course self-separating. And to say that it is only for artistic purposes is a mere begging of the question. Only four or five of these columns are complete, and a footing of the numbers in each gives us varying amounts from 113 to 153, and tells us nothing. On the parts that are left we six times have a Chuen with a black number apparently belonging to it (perhaps a multiplier), and also once a double Chuen, as in Tro.-Cort. The use of the red *kal*-sign, or 20, is frequent.

The lower division of these pages was also subdivided, into four sections on each, which we may refer to as *d, e, f, g*. Each contains a picture, with black and red numerals as above, surmounted by four glyphs only. The pictures are all quite incomplete; neither is there anything to add to what has been already said of the glyphs.

In the middle of page 17 one tonalamatl ends, with a red 6, and another begins, also with 6. The second starts with the day 6 Oc, is divided into fifths, and the initial column must have been in full: 6 Oc, Ik, Ix, Cimi, Ezanab. The restoration of the series gives: $6^{22}2^{(15 \text{ in two stages})}(4)^{10}1^46$. This however only gives a total of 51 for the black counters. There is space to the right for another section, but whatever may have been written there has entirely disappeared. The last three numbers 1^46 seem unmistakable, the ●●●● especially so. If we regard the last 6 as an error for 5, and then restore ^{16} in section 18-g, it would give the necessary 52. This is the one passage in the Codex where I can see no way but to assume a mistake in the writing; for 1 plus 4 does not equal 6, and unless for some entirely unknown reason the error is clear.

The preceding tonalamatl may have been divided either into 52- or 65-day periods. If the period was 52, it must have begun with an initial column on page 15, right side. In this event it would be restored as follows:

$$(\text{initial } 6)^{(19 \text{ in two stages})}(12)^{65}7 12^{(12 \text{ in two stages})}(11)^86,$$

giving 52. In this case a third tonalamatl must have begun somewhere to the left, and ended on the erased right side of page 15.

A different restoration would carry the initial column back to the extreme edge of page 15, when we would have this:

$$(\text{initial } 6)^{(2)}(8)^83^{11}(1)^{(11 \text{ in two stages})}(12)^{65}7 12^{(12 \text{ two stages})}(11)^86$$

giving 65.

To choose between these two would be mere guessing.

The well-known pages 19 and 20 come next. Together they make four compartments, up and down the full length of the pages, two with red and two with black backgrounds. Each is, or rather was, preceded by a column of 13 "year-bearers." The left column on each page I have restored, although no traces of it are left. But apart from its manifest necessity, as part of the series, if the width of the red ground on page 20 (see the photographs) is measured, it will be found to be just the correct proportion, and part of the straight left edge of the red can still be seen, just left of the rod in the hand of the mummy-figure, and leaving just room for the Ezanab column. In the colored plates I have only shown 12 instead of 13 day-signs in each column, but a measurement of the space above and below shows that the missing four are to be placed at the top and not at the bottom. These two pages therefore have application in some way to 52 solar years, beginning with 1 Lamat and ending with 13 Akbal (Votan).

These "year-bearers" are those of the Tzental instead of the Yucatecan system, as described by Landa, and on these two pages rests, so far as regards known subject-matter, the assignment of the Codex Perez to the Palenque rather than to the northern Maya district. It is thus to be considered with the Inscriptions of that region, and with the Dresden Codex.[5] And in accord with what is known of the state of the different parts of the country at the time of the Conquest, and of the history of the break-up and extinction of the Maya empire, it must be assigned the greater antiquity on that account.

It is probable that pages 19 and 20 had no text passages.

Pages 21 and 22 again, judging from the coloring and the arrangement, seem to form a pair. Each had on the upper part probably five rows of glyphs, some 70 in all, of which only 10 or 12 are at all recognizable. Contrary to all the pages hitherto discussed, it may be that these glyphs are to be *read from right to left*. The faces in these all look to the right, and the customary prefixes are all on the right. In classifying these glyphs, therefore, they must be all reversed.

The greater part of page 21 is framed in and divided up by green bands, evidently for water, two branches of which, after crossing a constellation band near the bottom, end one in falling torrents, the other in a circle surrounding a *kin*-sign, the sun, and itself surrounded by four dragon's heads, all figured in the midst of the torrents. Below this symbol is the open mouth of a dragon, towards which is looking and pointing a black-faced figure, of the god D, the Ancient of Days, described by Schellhas as the moon and night god. To the left of the torrents is a figure, nearly erased, but with the wristlets characteristic of the god of death, and holding in the hand a torch. The glyph occurs written in the torrents, at the left side.

The green bands divide the middle of the page into six compartments containing, so far as not totally erased, 65 day-signs, in columns of five. All my efforts to relate these signs either to each other or to any other series in the codices, have so far been fruitless. The upper seven columns have each a black numeral beneath, running from right to left, 1 2 3 3 5 6 and the dot of another 6.

Each of the columns of five day-signs forms a closed circuit returning into itself. In the upper row the 1st and 6th columns show successive days 8 apart in

[5] Where to place the Tro.-Cort., in view of the *apparent* Kan, Muluc Ix, Cauac years indicated on pages 34-37, and the 13 Cumhu immediately next to 13 Ahau on page 73 (13 Ahau 13 Cumhu falling only possibly in a year 12 Lamat) I am not ready to say.

order; columns 2, 3, 4, 5 and 7 are 16 apart in order. The 1st in the lower row is at intervals of 8, the 2nd and 5th at intervals of 16. The 3rd column is, with the 4th, an exception, the intervals being successively 8, 4, 4, 8, 16. That this is probably not a scribal error is shown by the fact that the same series, though beginning with different days, occurs in both columns. The 6th and possible 7th columns of the lower part are indeterminable.

We thus have three rounds of 5 times 8, or 40 days; seven rounds of 5 times 16, or 80 days; two irregular rounds of 40 days. These are not such columns as could form the beginning of a series of tonalamatl fifths, in which the successive days come 12 apart. So that this section must be left unexplained.[6]

At the right of page 21 begins a solid red background which probably extended right across page 22. Two standing spotted green figures appear on page 21; seven seated figures, one green spotted, on page 22.

Page 22 is crossed by a winding dragon whose body is covered by the "constellation band." A narrow green band also winds across the page, inclosing two of the upper figures. Below the dragon and this green band are seen, seated above the open mouths of two erect dragons, two figures in conversation, each bearing various insignia of the death god. A very curious cartouche outline, partly erased, at the lower right, incloses what seems to be 13 Ahau, 3, 6, the right hand dot of the 3 being erased.

On pages 23 and 24 the brilliant backgrounds of the preceding pages disappear, and we have two pages, to be read together, of glyphs, day-signs and small figures, finely and sparingly illuminated with the usual four colors. The body of the dragon is apparently continuous from page 21, and crosses these pages entirely with the constellation band, displayed along its full length.

The upper part of these two pages contained originally 91 glyphs, perhaps to be read *from right to left*, the same as 21 and 22. The faces look to the right, the usual *prefixes* and the few numerals are also on the right of their respective compounds. Many of the glyphs are the same as those on pages 2 to 11, reversed right for left. Glyph 23-a-11 should be specially noted. At first sight the numeral prefix, 6, appears to belong, postfixed, to glyph 23-a-17. But on investigation we find the same compound, a *yax-chuen* with ⬡ prefix, also at 21-a-8 and 24-a-26, in each case with the 6 attached. The ⬡ affix just below this number 6 is also plainly a *prefix* to glyph 23-a-12; so that glyph 23-a-ll must be read ⬡. and include the 6 as prefix. At 24-a-26, ⬡ the same glyph is written left ⬡ to right.

---

[6] Mr. Bowditch suggests to me that the numbers 1 2 3 3 5 6 6 are to be read with each of the day signs in their respective columns, and, being placed in the middle, may apply both to the upper and lower sets. The strongest objection I can see to this is that the numbers are black, instead of the usual red. In this case, instead of intervals of 8 and 16, giving rounds of 5×8=40 and 5×16=80 days, we would have intervals of 156 and 208 (from 1 Ymix to 1 Muluc, etc.), giving rounds of 780 and 1040 days respectively. Or, if read *upwards*, we would have 52 and 104 day intervals (1 Ben to 1 Chicchan, etc.), and rounds of 260 and 520 days. But whichever be the case, the page is *sui generis*, and its why is still beyond us.

There are also a few other glyphs on these pages which cannot be regarded as right to left. Such for instance, as   at 23-a-19 and 24-a-17. In this glyph the affix   at the side is properly a   prefix (perhaps the possessive), and I do not recall any instance of its use as a postfix. In the affixes, the superfix and prefix positions may as a general rule be regarded as wholly identical; also the subfix and postfix positions. But also as a general rule the two pairs are I believe not to be interchanged, any more than we interchange prefixes and endings in English; this rule is not universal for all affixes, as some seem able to go anywhere, but it is one I have always regarded in my glyph classifying. As to   it is to be noted that this is a symmetrical glyph and as there can be no doubt   that these glyphs were equally legible to the Maya reader written in either direction, it may well be regarded as unimportant, and not to be rated even as an error.   is a still stronger similar case. Here the wing affix to the right is certainly a   postfix, the superfix is in the usual left to right order,   and the main element written left to right, as in all its other instances. And   is again in point.

The face-*tun* compounds on these pages,   and also on the opposite side of the manuscript, should be particularly noted.

Below the constellation band, inscribed on a wavy green band (the waters of space?) are seven repetitions of   or the sun glyph   within the shields.[7] Between each appeared   probably two   black 8's. The sun-shields are about to be seized by different animals, dragon, tortoise, bird, etc., a seeming evident suggestion of either an eclipse, or the passage of the sun into some zodiacal sign. Another series of seven sun-shields, on the green band, separated by numeral 8's, and attacked by animals and a skeleton, crosses the lower part of the pages.

Between these two bands we find a series of columns of five day-signs each preceded by red numerals. Allowing for the space erased I have restored the last column to the right, and part of the preceding. This gives 12 columns only, whereas at least 13 are required. There may have been a 12th column to the left of page 23, where there is just the proper space for this,[8] leaving the dragon's body to curve above the column so as to pass to page 22. The series may have continued on across page 25; 13 columns on pages 23, 24, and 7 more filling page 25, would make a full cycle of 20 columns. And in this connexion it should be noted that the dragon's body with constellation band goes almost to the edge of page 24 with no sign of ending or turning, such as might be expected if the chapter ends here. And if the constellation dragon continues over page 25, the column series may well have done the same.

Before discussing this series it will be of advantage to review what the Codex

---

[7] I have retained the usual term "shields" for the flaring forms which embrace the sun glyph, though without accepting its appropriateness. They might with equal likelihood be conventionalized wings.

[8] Dr. Förstemann ignores the space on the right of page 24, and restores two columns to the left of page 23 in order to make up the thirteen columns; but, as shown by the edges of the pages in the photographs, one column restored in each place will just fill the obliterated space.

gives us on the question of reading left to right or right to left.

First, in both the Dresden and Tro.-Cort. the glyph faces look to the left; and, as shown by the calculations, reading is from left to right, with a very few possible exceptions, such as the tables on Dres. 24, 64, 69, etc.

In the Perez, as shown by the tonalamatls on 15 to 18, the 52 year-bearers on 19 and 20, and the katun-series on 2 to 12, the general direction of the reading is also left to right.

Above or below each of the red number columns of these pages 23, 24, is to be found a blue number. These numbers make a katun-series, starting with 4, decreasing by 2, if we read it left to right. It is not, to be sure, accompanied by the customary Ahau-sign, , but, taken in connexion with the marked parallelism of the glyphs, face-tun glyphs and also others, on these two pages with those on pages 2 to 11, already discussed, the possibility that a katun-series is a part of this subject-matter must be considered.

On the other hand, the glyphs in the upper part of all four pages 21 to 24 face to the right, and, as already set out in detail, are practically all written in *reverse position* as regards their prefixes, etc. And so also does the Eb-glyph in the day-columns we are now considering face to the right. These columns, unlike those on page 21, which include all of the 20 day-signs, only include 5 of the day-signs: Kan, Lamat, Eb, Cib and Ahau; Eb being the only non-symmetrical one of these.

We have thus quite strong evidence, especially as provided by the position of the prefixes, for a right to left reading, opposed by the direction of this katun-number series—if it be one. In Egyptian writing, of course, the direction of the reading changes with the facing of the figures.

To return now to the columns themselves, all the day-signs in any one column have each the same red numeral, so that we have: 8 Cib, 8 Ahau, 8 Kan, 8 Lamat, 8 Eb; and so on. The red numerals to each column also decrease by 2 towards the right, pari passu with the blue numerals. If we read each column downwards, it will form a closed circuit or round, returning into itself, with intervals of 104 days, from 8 Cib to 8 Ahau, etc., and again from 8 Eb back to 8 Cib. But if we next try to go to the next column, the series breaks, for from 8 Eb to 6 Lamat is only 76 days. We get a like break whether we read upward or downward, or right to left. Taking the columns separately then, the entire series (whether made up of 13, 20 or any other number of columns) cannot be made to read in one regular series, with a constant interval between the successive days of the whole.

But, if we restore two columns, making 13 columns, and then read horizontally *across*, either right to left, or left to right, one line after another, the first day of the second line follows the last of the first, and after going through the whole 65 terms, we return again from the last of the last line to the first of the first—always with a constant interval. In other words, this section could be written around a wheel. If we read left to right, the distance from (10 Kan) to 8 Cib, etc., is 232 days; 232×65=15,080. Or if from right to left,[9] the interval from (12 Lamat) to 1 Cib, etc., is 28 days; 28×13 = 364, ×5 = 1820. That both of these products are multiples of 260

[9] Dr. Seler's reading; *Gesammelte Abhandlungen*, I, 515.

is a truism, and cannot in any way require us to see a tonalamatl reckoning as the basis of this passage. Nor is each separate day-column a tonalamatl in fifths, as so often found.

Finally, if we should assume that the series went on across page 25, to a full katun-round of 20 terms, the circuit would be broken; line 2 would not regularly follow line 1, and so on. The probabilities then, as derived from the succession of the days, seem almost conclusive that this is a section of 65 terms, to be read horizontally, in whichever direction. And then, since the subdivision of 15,080 days (or 1820, if read right to left) into 65 terms, *necessarily* gives us successive day-*numbers* decreasing (or increasing) by 2, the likeness to the katun-series may be only apparent—a simple truism. Or, on the other hand, in view of the glyph similarities (a point which I think should always be given close attention), there *may* be some relation to the katun-series—all in spite of the right-left or left-right difficulties.

What part the blue[10] number series plays, I cannot say. Dr. Seler,[11] suggests that they are "corrections," to set each term ahead 20 days. This states a fact, but does not give any explanation. Each blue number is 6 less than its red column, and 7 Kan *is* of course 20 days later than 13 Kan.

---

[10] The blue is a true blue, quite distinct from the turquoise blue elsewhere, and is found in the case of these numbers only.

[11] *Gesammelte Abhandlungen*, I, 515; "Zur mexik. Chronologie."

THE MAYA GLYPHS

Up to date our knowledge of the meanings of the glyphs is still to all intents and purposes limited to the direct tradition we have through Landa, and the deductions immediately involved in these. We know the day and month signs, the numbers, including 0 and 20, four units of the archaic calendar count (the day, tun, katun and cycle), the cardinal point signs, the negative particle. We have not fully solved the uinal or month sign, which seems to be *chuen* on the monuments and a *cauac*, or *chuen*, in the manuscripts. We are able to identify what must be regarded as metaphysical or esoteric applications of certain glyphs in certain places, such as the face numerals.[12] But every one of these points is either deducible directly by necessary mathematical calculation, or else from the names of certain signs given by Landa in his day and month list, and then found in other combinations, such as *yax*, *kin*, etc. That we have as many of the points as we have, and still cannot form from them the key—that we cannot *read* the glyphs—is a constant wonder; but a fact nevertheless.

The innumerable efforts to identify the glyphs by their superficial appearance, calling the banded headdress a "pottery decoration," and explaining the face-glyph of the North thereby, because in Maya *xaman* is north and *xamach* a tortilla dish (to say nothing of others still more fanciful, by a host of writers), have broken down, as was to be expected. I mention this instance because it illustrates fully the results of superficial analysis, united with a seeming ineradicable tendency even among those most able students who have added the most to our stock of Maya knowledge (among whom Dr. Brinton was certainly one of the foremost), to treat these glyphs as carelessly done, to disregard the differences between manifest variants, or else to talk freely, whenever a passage does not fit the explanation which is being worked out, of scribal errors.

In the first place, *if* these glyphs are to be interpreted primarily by the Yucatecan Maya dialect (one in which we have most ample printed and MS. lexicographic material), and if in that dialect no other words at all resembling *xaman* and *xamach* are found, as we are told, then (*if* the Mayas named the north star, or the North, by a pun on a tortilla dish) wherever this banded headdress is found, we must assume the text to be treating either of the North, or of tortillas. That might safely be left to break down of its own weight; but we shall also see that the explanation is given in total disregard of manifest, important variants. This banded headdress appears

---

[12] The Tibetan use of symbolical words in place of numerals is worth noting here, even though we do not know the Maya face numerals well enough as yet for any comparison. See Csoma de Kőrös, *Tibetan grammar*, Calcutta, 1824, pp. 155 *et seq.*; also Ph. Éd. Foucaux, *Grammaire Tibétaine*, Paris, 1858, pp. 157 *et seq.*

ornamenting at least five separate and distinct faces; one a wholly human face, the others with various other definite characteristics, the most frequent and prominent of which are the monkey-like face and mouth we see in the glyph for the north, and a sort of bird's plumage covering the back of the head. These two are separate, are never combined, and must be classified rigidly apart. We have therefore three elements, the monkey face, the plumage covering (if we may call it so), and the banded headdress. It is obvious that while the monkey face may be specific of the North, the bands are not specific at all, but general.

It is with the greatest diffidence that I suggest any interpretations on my own part as yet, but it is of course certain that the distinction of masculine and feminine existed in the spoken language, and it must exist somewhere in the glyphs. And it will have to be a prefix, not a postfix; for what I may call the syntax of glyph formation must follow that of the speech. At the bottom of Dres. 61 and 62 are seven identical Oc-glyphs with subfix, and with prefixes. Five of these prefixes are faces with the woman's curl, recognized on the figured illustrations. One is a face with the banded headdress. Remembering that this headdress occurs not infrequently on a plain human face with no other characteristic, it is not a far guess that it may have denoted a freeman, a lord, entitled to such a headdress. In this event it may on the one hand serve as a simple masculine definitive, the prefix *ah-*, and on the other, to attach the idea of lordship to other glyphs with which it is incorporated, as: the North Star, or region, the Lord of the Firmament.

This illustration serves to show what seems to me an essential preliminary of the work we have in hand, and the part to which I have so far devoted most effort. The glyphs must be determined, compared and classified, and what I have called the "syntax" of their composition, studied. The particles and their positions, the various *incorporated* elements, are of the utmost importance, though they are very frequently ignored. *They are the written picture of the spirit of the spoken language.* The task I have most looked forward to in this connexion has of course been with the Dresden, but having started upon the Perez for the reasons I have given, it was a smaller task in itself, and could be brought to completion within less time, while serving as part of the larger work. As the determination and classification of the glyphs had to proceed all as one work, it has enabled me not only to complete my Index for this codex, but also to print the text in type, and to verify and bring out such facts regarding the color questions as was possible to do—both of them stages needed in the general work. In doing it I have studied with my hands as well as with eyes, and I have been well repaid. The actual labor has not been small, but it has been worth it all if only to see before the eyes something of what this Codex must have been when fresh and new. For as I have said, while in my colored restoration I may have made some mistakes of eye, for which the photographs will be a check, I have *guessed* nothing.

The classification of the glyphs meets of course with some difficulties in detail, but it can readily be cast into a quite simple general outline. Something over 2000 different compound forms are found in the three codices. The simple elements composing these are perhaps 350 in number, and may be divided broadly into main elements and affixes or particles. First of course come day and month signs, which, with *kin, tun, kal,* and a few marked variants, use up 50 numbers. Next will come the faces, about 75 simple elements. Next the animal and bird heads and figures, about 50 numbers. Next the hands, crosses, etc., and the list of conventional or geometric forms, another 75. Then some 75 particles.

The cards required for the first 50 numbers, including only compounds formed from day-signs and excluding day-signs used simply as such, amount to practically one half of the number required for the whole index. Certain elements, notably the *kin,* the *tun,* the monkey-face with banded headdress, already referred to, the face with tau-eye, the *yax,* the cross, produce a great number of compounds—a fact of note, as it is evident that the number of compounds, having due regard to our limited material, is an index to the relative position of the idea in the Mayan vocabularies. Some of the day-signs produce practically no compounds, others a great many. The compounds fall readily into a system of primary and secondary derivatives, by which their relations may be easily studied, and their proportions recognized.

Coming to the distinguishing of variants, one first meets the fact that the three codices differ. The writing of the Dresden and Perez is regular and accurate, the Perez exceedingly so. Every different variant must here be accounted for. In Tro.-Cort. the writing is crude and careless, so that we have many evident abbreviations which are not genuine variants. In the next place, certain regular differences occur in this or that glyph or particle, between the forms of the different manuscripts. Thus the Perez uses ▭ and the others ▭ and so on. A comparison of the compounds shows that these must be the same. The regular variations between the three manuscripts and variations of abbreviation, when well evidenced, may be eliminated.

The day-signs have many variants, mostly quite simple, and all checked positively by the use of the form in some day-series. Ix has many forms. There are at least three entirely different Cimi forms: There are found two different forms of the closed eye, one of which certainly is Cimi, the other occurs regularly in such different compounds (and I think never as a simple day-sign), as to make it necessary to separate it; it has probably a different meaning entirely—perhaps that of sleep.

A noteworthy technical line is to be found in the drawing of the glyphs. Whereas in the case of the day-signs, faces, and conventional forms in general, certain variations of handwriting, etc., are evidently permitted, but only within certain definite lines, in some few animal glyphs no two instances are just alike. In other words, the glyphs in general are conventions with established meanings—actual writing;[13] but we also have *pictures* of birds or animal forms, where the writer is not following convention, but nature. The freedom of style used in the

[13] "These [the Maya glyphs] do not represent a real script, as is so often maintained, but are only pictures which have been reduced to the appearance of letters, contracted to a narrow space, made cursive."!—Dr. Eduard Seler, *Codex Vaticanus No. 3773,* page 65.—Well?

latter case only serves to emphasize the conventionality of the former, and to separate the entire system from either picture or rebus writing. See the following fish-glyph forms:

These pictures are almost exclusively in uncompounded forms, whereas the conventional glyphs, whether human, animal or otherwise, are subject to the general rules of incorporation.

Writing is a system of conventional forms with established meanings, corresponding to and reflecting the structure of the spoken language; some picture elements whose value as such has remained either wholly or partly present in the minds of those who use them, are not inconsistent with genuine writing; when present they add vividness to the writing, and emphasize its ideographic character. A combination of picture forms only, may be used as means of communication to a certain degree, but can never constitute *writing*; that, like speech, must provide for the expression of the relationships and categories that make up the structure of language.

Egyptian writing, which is of course *true writing*, contains elements of every class. It has symbols and also pictures, not only of things or creatures, but of actions as well, "contracted to a narrow space, made cursive"; these pictures, although still ranking as such, stand for *words*—they can be *pronounced*, and have syntax, which is the crucial test. Egyptian next has unrecognizable forms, whose meaning has become a simple convention, but which still stand for *words*, or particles. It has elements which are not pronounced for themselves, but only serve as determinatives. (Such a use of determinatives is not limited to hieroglyphic writing, but is possessed also by alphabetic; the second *o* in the word *too* is strictly a determinative, to distinguish the adverb *too* from the preposition *to*, both pronounced alike. Tibetan has an elaborate system of silent letters used as grammatical determinatives.) And then Egyptian writing finally has pure alphabetic elements.

As to Maya, I think it far more than likely that, when at last deciphered, it will be found to contain most if not all of these classes—*mutatis mutandis*. There seems every evidence that it is made up of pictures with probably both concrete and abstract meanings; word-conventions; and grammatical particles. It is at least probable that there are also silent determinatives and not unlikely that there is also a pure phonetic or alphabetic element. That the latter element is not the basic one may I think be now regarded as established.

CONCLUSION

Introite, nam et hic dii sunt.

It is not my desire to add, as a conclusion to a comment bearing on the restoration and interpretation of Mayan hieroglyphic texts, any general discussion of the data which tradition and the early Spanish writers have left us of the mythology, rites and customs of the American races; and still less to run out a line of attractive analogies between isolated instances of their words, symbols or works, with those of any of the various nations of the other hemisphere; nor to build up any theory of descent or intercourse with any of these latter as today known to history. The subject before us is on its very face too vast; the written and traditional data are entirely too scanty and too little understood; and while we are still obliged to designate the various gods and personages of the Codices as god A, B, etc., and are unable to fix definitely[14] a single inscribed date in terms of our chronology, or tell the event attached to it, fancied comparisons amount to little. And the favorite "linguistic" method is more fragile yet, especially when the uncertainties of spelling and transliteration are considered, and above all the frequent total ignorance of the past history and changes the different words

---

[14] See *Memoranda on the Chilam Balam Calendars*, C. P. Bowditch, 1901. The obscurities of the Chronicles render the questions connected with Ahpula's death exceedingly difficult. For instance, the immediate context in the books of Mani and Tizimin make the date 1536, as given in numerals, an impossible one. But, if the date as given in *Maya terms* is to be accepted at all (and it certainly is too specific to be rejected), then by the long count such a date *must* have been either 1502, 5350, or 12,786 years after the date of Stela 9, Copan. Mr. Bowditch favors the lower figure, chiefly because it is the lower, and thus puts Stela 9 at A. D. 34. To get this date the longest possible distance from Ahpula's death to the end of the katun must be used—that is, "6 tuns short" must be taken to mean "almost 7 tuns short." I can only say here that if, in correcting the figures 1536, as demanded by the immediate context, we make the simplest possible correction, and put them one katun earlier, 1516, and then take as the unexpired time to the end of the katun the shortest of the three terms given as possible, or 5 tuns 139 days, bringing the end of Katun 13-Ahau on Jan. 28, 1522, we not only bring the end of Katun 11-Ahau within the year 1541, as is most positively stated by the practically contemporary Pech Chronicle, but we also bring in line nearly all the important events of the Chronicles, from the fall of Mayapan, ca. 1450, the coming of the Spaniards, and the smallpox, in 11-Ahau (1521 to 1541), the conversion to Christianity in 9-Ahau, down to Landa's death (1579) in 7-Ahau; as well as many outside references. Any other combination requires harsher emendations somewhere else. But the above choice of the term of 5 tuns 139 days, thus seemingly called for, means that Stela 9 at Copan is dated, by the long count, 5350 years before Ahpula's death, or B. C. 3824. Whether this is right, is a question for the future.

compared must have gone through since the time when by any possibility a physical transmission from one locality to the other could have taken place. These ought to be commonplaces of research, but it is to be feared that they have not quite yet become so.[15] There is no need to give instances of such false analogies which have served as the bases for a multitude of filiation theories, all equally well "supported" by details, and all mutually exclusive. Nor on the other hand can we deny the existence actually of a very great number of resemblances and identities which cannot be ignored, but must imply connexions of some kind. The English nation is not a Hebrew people because it had a prime minister Disraeli, nor Greeks because they have a Queen Alexandra, nor Romans because of certain local names. Such facts even when real, and established as such, may only be evidence of a single continental culture or transcontinental intercourse.

It has been the dictum of a certain school of archaeology, still very much in general favor, that all these identities are to be explained as the natural result of the innate tendencies of untutored men, on their evolutionary rise, at certain cultural stages, to imagine the same myths and invent the same rites. From this as a principle I wholly dissent; it simply does not meet the facts. There are of course many facts to which it does apply, such as those that both Chinese and Americans made paper, tanned leather, made feather ornaments, used star and flower names for their children, and so on: facts which had been used to prove Chinese and American identity, and to which Dr. Brinton justly added in retort that they also slept at night, wore clothes when it was cold, and so on. But there is a very great number of facts, a number constantly growing with research, which cannot be so dismissed. Such are the employment of abstract symbolism, the erection of great structures all having a definite and identical astronomical bearing and evident use, the common possession of so-called myths all telling the one story, and only slightly modified locally, such as the birth-stories of Huitzilopochtli and of Herakles, and the stories of the travail of Latona pursued by the Python and of the Woman clothed with the Sun in *Revelation*; or the universal tradition of seven ancestral caves or cities in America, compared with the Tibetan and Purânic stories

---

[15] "In ethnology however one troubles oneself little with the detail of linguistic structure. It is held quite sufficient to gather from different peoples and collate a couple of hundred vocables, into whose actual nature all insight is lacking, and then upon dubious, often purely superficial and apparent similarities, to deduce linguistic affinities. Or else, as is now most in fashion, the claims of linguistic research towards the solution of ethnological questions are reduced to a 'most modest share' in comparison with other fields 'somewhat more in line with natural sciences'—meanwhile pointing for justification to the absurdities set forth as the results of too far-fetched linguistic deductions.... The errors and sophistries charged against ethnological linguistics are rather an accidental result of the individuality of single investigators, than essential to the subject. They are at least scarcely greater than those to the credit of recent Anthropometry. A brief glance at the strange changes of opinion in the latter field during the last three decades, in spite of all its boasted figures, shows how little ground it has to throw stones. Serious students, such as Wallace and Dall, whose critical ability in Zoomorphology no one can deny, and who do not rest content with a few skulls of doubtful *provenance*, gathered à la Hagenbeck, have come to a wholly negative view of the value of Craniometry."—Dr. Otto Stoll, *Maya-Sprachen der Pokom-Gruppe*, I, vii, ix.

of the seven lotus-leaves of Śveta-dvîpa, the first continental home of the race; the *Hacha de cobre* of the Miztecs and the ever-turning spear of jade of the Japanese story of the place where the gods first descended on earth; or the whole question of the origin of the Zodiac. These things, and a host of others, need a different explanation—all the more since the more we are learning of them the more we find that they enclose facts of which the hypothetical "savage children" could not, *ex hypothesi*, have been aware—some facts indeed which our very latest modern science is only now learning.[16]

But while dissenting now wholly from this theory (of "coincidentalism") one cannot but hold in all respect those who in their time held it. It is the duty of the savant to make the best logical use he can of what he has, and he cannot be criticised for not using finer scales than the time affords. And this theory was needed as an answer to the absurdities, brought out in utter disregard of physical possibilities, postulating off-hand migrations and filiations and evolutionary advances totally impossible within the periods allowed for their completion, and utterly without parallel in any known part of the world or page of history. And yet, when this theory had its birth, the most of Christendom was still enthralled by the Ussherian chronology of the creation and history of the whole divine universe, which simply did not have room in it for all these things to happen naturally and connectedly.

And if it is urged that present science had already say a generation ago, a second's time we might say in the life of humanity, begun to emancipate our ideas of time and evolution, still it is the fact that that increase in breadth of vision has so far applied to every known thing but man himself. The old belief that gave the world 6000 years of life, at least put thinking man at its beginning; the modern nightmare gives us a world for hundreds of millions of years without *thought*, and makes human civilization an ephemeral episode of a few seconds of universal duration. Disregarding, one is forced to say wilfully, the fact that every single one of their own arguments in favor of anthropoid descent for man would equally support a theory that the anthropoids are debased offshoots of human stocks,[17] biology still demands such a lapse of time for its physical evolution

---

[16] Our present day speculators never seem to think for a moment that these things may conceal, *and thereby preserve*, some real meaning, or be more than nonsense. The theory of mythological interpretation pushed to such extremes as in the "animistic" *explanations* of Weber, Keightley, and others, and not absent from the writings of some Americanists (namely, that it was all nothing but ridiculous or concocted fancy, taken soberly) is bad enough, and argues little breadth or insight, when applied to the myths of a single people, considered alone. Applied to comparative mythology, in the state of things today, it is simply impossible. The plain fact is, that such identities as these must indicate one of two things: a common tradition, locally modified by circumstances; or a *fact in nature* or *history*, symbolically expressed in different ways according to the times and modes. And it most probably indicates both of these. It is indeed hard to account for the extent, and the weight given to some of these "myths," now that we are coming to a better appreciation of the scope and greatness of ancient civilizations—everywhere—except they do correspond to actual *facts* in nature and history. And it might be worth our while to get at some of these.

[17] We might just as well acknowledge, once for all, that in spite of its present-day currency in England and America, and its pre-emption of the field of "science for the people," the theory of man's physical and mental descent from the anthropoids, is not only *not*

that its adherents oppose and belittle to the utmost every bit of evidence of any antiquity even for the physical frame of man. We have, to say nothing of the rest of the world, Egyptian civilization now pushed back 10,000 years, and (together with others as we slowly uncover them) as far removed as ever from barbarism, if not indeed growing greater as we go back; but we are not allowed anything but apelike, half arboreal savages 50,000 years ago. And yet every observed *fact* shows us savage or worn-out races everywhere throughout the world deteriorating and dying out, and nowhere any savages progressing or, unaided by outside influence, developing what we know as civilization. We see everywhere the rise and fall of nations, races and civilizations, and their utter blotting out; and we refuse to accept that process as a universal law through which the destiny of the human race is working itself out. In fact, we do not seem to believe that the human race has any destiny; it may have beginning and an end, but no destiny.

And so although this modern scientific school began as a reaction against the narrowness of theological limitations, both of time and greatness, so hampered *proved*, but is vehemently denied by an equally able and scientific, and withal more logical, body of researchers than those who form its supporters. To *fabricate* a missing link in a chain (or even, as with Haeckel, several links), whose only authority is acknowledged to be its necessity in order to complete the evidence for the theory, and then to declare the theory proved because the fabricated link fits perfectly the gap it was created for, is equally vicious scientifically whether the fabrication be the work of a physicist of renown or a linguistic theorizer. Let it simply be agreed, as it now is by all science, that the *evolution of form* is a universal and well evidenced principle, working out through the various well established and comprehensible incidents, such as natural selection, adaptation to environment, and so on—yet this statement of the fact is not an explanation of its cause. And every scientific and logical requirement will be equally, and better, met by regarding all forms, whether physical, linguistic, or of any kind, as coming, or rather brought, into being by the force of a consciousness which needs them as the vehicles of its expanding activity. That this is absolutely true in language, anybody can see. That it is true in every department of daily life about us, everybody *does* see. That it should be equally true in biology and physics, would not affect the standing or verity of a single *observed* fact.

There was, along about the beginning of the Christian era, and for some time before and after, a very curious movement, which seemed to spread itself over nearly the entire world, east and west. It is told of the early Aztecs that "they destroyed the records of their predecessors, in order to increase their own prestige." It is related that writing once existed in Peru, but was entirely wiped out, and the Inca records committed to quipus alone. The "burning of the books" under Tsin Chi Hwangti in B. C. 213 sought to do the same for China. The times of Akbar witnessed much of the same in India. And in Europe almost nothing was left to tell the tale of the great pre-Christian eastern empires and systems of thought; so that from the establishment of State Christianity under Constantine, and the final settlement of the Canon at the Council of Nicaea, an impenetrable veil was drawn over the achievements and greatness of the Past, and all connexion therewith broken off. It was some time after this that we find the heliocentric theory, as well as that of other habitable worlds, denied (in Europe), because "it would deprive the Earth of its unique and central eminence." Just as we also today are served up with prehistoric savage and animal ancestors, to the greater glory of our own present-day magnificence. But it really is in sober truth only a question of mental perspective which does not affect the facts of history, biology, archaeology or language in the least. It is only a question of which end of the telescope we look through.

and hypnotized has our thought been by both, that man is of nearly as little universal account with one as with the other, and we find a seemingly ineradicable repugnance to admit that any people had "developed" writing before the least possible time ago we can fix it, usually this side of the year 1 of the Christian era. And thus we have M. Terrien de Lacouperie's "450 *embryo* scripts and writings" — which another fifty years may show to be nearly as many fragments of one or a few great stocks of ancient hieroglyphs. Of course it is impossible to derive the American races or civilizations from the Chinese, Phoenicians, Hittites, or any of the cultures of the other hemisphere, if we limit the latter to what we know of their history within the past two or three thousand odd years, and American civilization to the past fifteen hundred years. The matter is somewhat greater than that—just as man is somewhat greater than a fool of natural caprice.

There is one point from which this question of American origins, at least of American place in human society and civilization, can be studied in its broader lines, even with what materials we have. It is that of language in general. All these other matters we have touched upon are necessary factors in the question of human evolution, and the position of America cannot be considered apart from them, and all of them. But Language touches both the glyphs directly and also all these other things, and is itself of surpassing interest and importance as a human study.

From one point of view Language is man himself, and it certainly is civilization. Without it man is not man, a Self-expressing and social being. It is, as von Humboldt laid down, not an act but an activity, or energy, not a thing done, but a doing. It is the constant effort of the conscious self to formulate thought. It is the use of the energy of creation, of objectivation, a veritable many-colored rainbow bridge between the inner or higher man and the outer or lower worlds. And it is not only the expression of Man as man, but in its varied forms it is the inevitable and living expression of each man or body of men at any and every point of time. Itself boundless as an ocean, it is in its infinite forms and streams and colors and sounds, the faithful and exact exponent both of the sources and channels by which it has come, and of the banks in which it is held, racial, national or individual. It is living or dead, forceful or weak, pure or foul, refreshing or flat, healing or poisonous. It limits us, but yields to our force. Every word or form comes to us with the thought impress of every man or nation that has used or molded it before us. We must take it as it comes, but we give it something of ourselves as we pass it on. If our intellectual and spiritual thought is aflame, whether as nation or individual, we may purify it, energize it, give it power to form and arrange the atoms around it—and we have a new literature, a new and beneficent, creative social vehicle of intercourse, mutual understanding, and human unification. Or if our mental or spiritual life is stale, and petty, or egoistic, or seeking for enjoyment only rather than action; if we have nothing in us to give the words and forms we use, but only some national force left to use and play with them, we for a while refine, and paint, and pettify, and elaborate into meaningless subtleties of form, every one of which in turn reacts upon our mental and spiritual life, distracting and enchaining us, until at last the nation and its language—die out; for neither can live without the other.

Now it is evident that the criterion of the perfectness of any language is not to be found in a comparison of its forms or methods with those of any other, but in its fitness as a vehicle for the expression of deeper life, of the best and the greatest that is in those who use it, and above all in its ability to react and stimulate newer and yet greater mental and spiritual activity and expression. The force behind man, demanding expression through him, and him only, into the human life of all, is infinite—of necessity infinite. There is no limit, nor ever has been any limit, to what man may bring down into the dignifying, broadening and enriching of human life and evolution, save in his own ability to comprehend, express, and *live* it. And the brightness and cleanness of the tools whereby he formulates his thought, as well as the worthiness and fitness of the substance and the forms into which he shapes it for others to see, are the essentials of his craft. For such is the economy of nature, which wastes nothing in reality, that a fit vehicle will be taken possession of by its own tenant; and the unfit left to and be taken by those who can use no better.

Before, then, taking up the great formal classes into which language at large is usually divided, it will be necessary to say a few words as to the foundations of form itself in language, that we may then proceed to consider these classes from the standpoint of their inner meaning rather than solely of the outer form; and by seeking to understand the mental and spiritual equipment and life of those that used them, may perhaps in turn be better fitted finally to enter into the genius of their written and spoken languages, and to interpret through them in the detail more of the ideas which those forms were both fitted and used to express. Such a method is essential for the understanding of any language or culture, but it is absolutely necessary in the case of these non-Aryan tongues, so great is the distance both of time and thought which separates us from them. If we set out to compare the forms by which they expressed their thought with those within which we develop ours, or approach these cultures and peoples in the attitude of alien criticism, study their "interesting ways" through a mental lorgnette and impale their dead forms on the needles of our collection, we shall not only show ourselves less broad in culture than many of them, but we shall simply close and lock the doors of discrimination and understanding before us. The question is not, How do their forms and ways appeal to us? but, How did those forms, and ways, achieve their underlying objects, and what was the *thought* behind them?

Life is action, and without activity whatever powers lie within any conscious being are only potential. Activity is the bridge between the inner man and the outer world, by which he impresses his thought, in forms, on chaos or the atoms about him, receiving in return increased knowledge and experience of all he touches, and knowledge of himself through the results of his own actions; and it is the bridge between man and man. For this reason the verb, the word of action, is the most important and most developed part of speech. The three hypostases of life, as of language, are the self, activity, and the world; and it is for the expression of all the possible varied relations between these three, that all the forms of any language come into being. And from the way in which these forms are developed, and the relative importance which is given to this or that form of thought or activity, the character of the people, their grasp of nature, and their own conception of themselves and their relation to the world, can be seen.[18] Some languages have the strong impress of impersonality, without any loss of virility; others are strongly egotistic and self-assertive, with perhaps the braggart's lack of genuine strength. Each spoken language that we know has its own color and tone, to which our thought must respond, if we would know and use it well. To

---

[18] It is exceedingly interesting to trace the course of criticism since the appearance of Wilhelm von Humboldt's great work, *Ueber die Verschiedenheit des menschlichen Sprachbaues und ihren Einfluss auf die geistige Entwickelung des Menschengeschlechts* (Berlin, 1836). Dr. Brinton gave it most unqualified approval; (see especially his monograph read before the American Philosophical Society in 1885, and printed the same year). Prof. H. Steinthal (*Grammatik, Logik und Psychologie*, 1855) calls the subject of "inner form" the most important one in linguistic science, and von Humboldt's treatment of it his greatest contribution to that science. And so on. But the work has nevertheless received little attention from a large number of writers, most of them declaring it "unclear." These two views, when one studies the various writers, seem to follow closely upon the standpoints from which each approaches the study. Those who study language (perhaps one should here say, languages) as a phenomenon, a set of external forms, an act, a thing done, get little use out of von Humboldt's work. Those who see it as a human "activity," an energy, get much. This is quite apparent in one of the clearest and ablest linguistic works which has recently appeared, Dr. Adolf Noreen's *Vårt Språk* (in 9 vols., still in course of publication, Lund, 1903 and later), a work of far wider linguistic value than appears from its title. Dr. Noreen, however, dismisses von Humboldt's work, and the subject of "inner form," with a few pages, and the results are apparent in several interesting points. In the first place, in the course of an acute and critical analysis, wherein he shows that the purpose of speech is not simply *expression* of thoughts or ideas, but the communication to some other person of the *knowledge* of the ideas so held by the speaker, he goes on to say: "the same knowledge of A's wishes could be as well communicated by his saying 'I want you to come' as by his saying just 'Come.'" This is quite true; but the *energic* effect is quite different. Language is the bridge from man to man, and it is also a *creative activity* of man. Of course Dr. Noreen, in a later volume, where he most lucidly analyses the terms 'words,' 'forms,' and 'concepts,' etc. (*ord, morfem, semem*, etc.), and corrects many errors of definition made by his predecessors, acknowledges the difference between the two forms; still his whole admirable work, analytical and critical as it is, is devoted to this phase of language as a mere phenomenon, a set of forms which serve as a medium of communication. From this standpoint, we know all there is to know about language when we have classified its forms. But from the other, the study is ever leading us into the regions and depths of man's consciousness, his creative activity as it goes out to the world; and the true definition of language, from this position, "can hence only be a genetic one." (von Humboldt, *Gesammelte Werke*, VI, 42)

It is further not unworthy of note that, except where directly required in treating of verbal categories, nearly all of the enormous number of illustrations which Dr. Noreen chooses for his points, are *nouns*, names of *things*, and vary rarely verbal forms, words of action and *doing*. But it is simply a fact that all the *potency* of language is in the verb, and almost all there is of language, in a philosophic sense, lies there. The verb is the bridge of communication and action *upon* external things, just as is language itself, going out of man. And it is also noteworthy that the recognition of this position of the verb, together with these other matters of which we are speaking, seems nearer at hand and clearer to those students who are led beyond Aryan languages to the study of American and Asiatic, especially Central and Northern Asiatic. For instance, G. v. d. Gabelentz, *Die Sprachwissenschaft*, and other works.

speak good Swedish, for instance, requires clear thinking to an exceptional degree. To show this, the form "come here," which is the ordinary English expression, is simply *bad grammar* in Swedish; the use of "come *hither*" (*kom hit*, instead of *kom här*) is imperative. We have the "hither" in English, but it has become stilted, and the linguistic distinction lost. Compare also the use of *få*, as a common auxiliary; nor are these exceptions, but, on the contrary, characteristic examples. Also to enunciate the language rightly one must hold the back and neck erect and the muscles firm.

In some languages the speaker thinks of himself and his completed action as inseparable, as a single idea, as the Latin *edi* for I have eaten; in others he thinks of himself subconsciously as possessing the results of his action, as our *I have eaten*; and in others, as among the Irish peasantry, he separates himself and his action entirely, as *I am after eating*. In some grammars, as in Maya, the verbal concept starts with the past; in others, as our own, we live in the present; in the Welsh, the future is the chief tense. The mere choice of *shall* or *will* as the first person future auxiliary denotes a specific mental quality.

Now the expression of all these infinite shades of relationship between the self, the activity and the world, is achieved in two ways: position or placement—syntax; and form. The customary division of languages is into Monosyllabic, Agglutinative, Incorporating, and Inflectional, and this division will suit our purpose, though it must be used with care. It is held in the ordinary theory that these classes must represent successive stages of linguistic perfection, each in turn being higher in the scale than the other, they having grown one from the other as the race advanced. By the theory the monosyllabic is lower than the agglutinative, and inherently less useful. But the theory does not work out in practical application to the facts we have to deal with, for while we cannot find still left in the world any agglutinative languages representative of sufficient culture to bring into our present consideration, we do find a monosyllabic in the highest rank, and meeting the highest cultural requirements. In short, the latter may be theoretically the inferior tool, but the genius of thought behind is greater than the form. One man can draw a masterpiece with a burnt stick, another only paint a daub with all the brushes made. Once again we must not judge by our preconceived preferences of form.

Omitting therefore the modern remnants of agglutinating languages, outside of America, as affording us no literary material of value for our study, we shall find at once drawn across all the other great classes a single broad line of division, between the ideographic and the literal—the same as already mentioned. And the moment we draw this line as an exponent of the mental and spiritual thought-life of the different peoples, we shall find it not only molding their language forms, both written and spoken, but manifest as well in their art, philosophy, and even their social polity. And of course we must be fair in our comparisons, and not set a Chinese coolie in the concrete against an English statesman, nor any concrete example of another kind of culture in its decay with the highest bloom to which we believe our own type to be able to carry us.

It would be absurd to say that the ratiocinative, literal mind is higher than the ideal. One man sees directly the meaning of the things, the events and situations before him; another reasons it all out. And contrary to many of our current beliefs, the former is often the man of action; he sees at a flash to the heart of the matter, and gets things done. His thought, his activity, is vivid; and his words are likely to be so as well. The idealist, if he be broadminded, and not merely sentimental, is indeed likely to be the practical man. And the type of mind that is made manifest to us by these great non-Aryan languages and their forms, is the former. Of course idealism in its decadence becomes negative, inactive, self-consuming and no longer creative. But in its bloom the direct vision may be even more active, more practical, than are the reasoned processes.

Much ink and paper has been spent over the question whether the Chinese hieroglyphs are ideograms or phonograms, whether the character 天, for instance, conveys to those using it primarily the idea of Heaven, or the spoken word *T'ien*. It is necessarily both, in a sense; it would not be written language otherwise. And it is equally true that the letter-combination *Heaven* is in a way as much to us a picture of the idea as of the sound; but the difference of procedure is radical. The glyph is related to the idea directly, the spelled word only through the formal combination of symbols for single vocal speech-elements, meaningless when separate. The relation of spoken sound to glyph is wholly adventitious; the relation of the idea to the spelled word is equally adventitious. The ascent, if we so call it, of written speech from the ideographic to the alphabetic, is the descent of the thought further into material forms.[19] And while it may be (and in the course of universal evolution rightly so) necessary for our thought to descend into the bondage of matter and form, for its knowledge and experience, and for the development of matter and form into fitter vehicles of thought, nevertheless the process is a binding and for a time an enchaining one, and the thought is, for a time at least, likely to be lost in the confusion of forms.

Thus we may lay down as our fundamental proposition that a hieroglyphic form of writing is better fitted to, and must properly, in the period of its natural development, accompany the imaginative processes of mind. Or, since imagination to our literal thought implies in some degree the fanciful (though wrongly so in

---

[19] It was not until after this paper was already in type that my attention was directed to the complete agreement of this and the succeeding sentences with the following passage in *The Secret Doctrine*, by H. P. Blavatsky, London, 1888, vol. II, page 199. After saying that some of the Atlantean races spoke the agglutinative languages, the passage continues: "While the 'cream' of the Fourth Race *gravitated* more and more toward the apex of physical and intellectual evolution, *thus* leaving as an heirloom to the nascent Fifth (the Aryan) Race the inflectional, highly developed languages, the agglutinative decayed and remained as a fragmentary fossil idiom, scattered now, and nearly limited to the aboriginal tribes of America." Note the words I have italicized, marking the evolution of the "inflectional" languages as an attendant phenomenon on physico-intellectual evolution, compare the passage with von Humboldt's thesis, already quoted, that the incorporative quality denotes an exaltation of the imaginative over the ratiocinative processes of mind in its users, and further with the surviving genius of Chinese, the type of monosyllabic languages, and the agreement is evident. Von Humboldt, however, did not carry out so fully the archaeological results, for which indeed the materials were in his day still lacking. See also other passages in *The Secret Doctrine*.

essence), we might perhaps better say that that form of writing is the fit attendant and exponent of those functions of mind which cognize the inner meanings of the facts of life directly, rather than those which study them through the correlation of their phenomena. And also, that the development by any people of an alphabetic out of a hieroglyphic system, does not imply a greater advance in linguistic perfection on their part, but indicates a corresponding mental and inner change of attitude towards ideas and things, and a different conception of the self as related to them all.

It is not at all necessary to assume that the knowledge gained by one method is deeper or more exact than the other. True science may exist as fully under one set of circumstances as the other. If we will take the type of the so-called most primitive form, the monosyllabic—the Chinese, we shall find all this evidenced in the clearest manner. To note but one illustration, a study of the scientific and philosophical ideas involved in and conveyed by the word *k'ung*, for Space, ether, the fundamental substratum of sound or vibration, as well as the "interetheric" central point of balance and power, will disclose an understanding that has nothing to fear from modern comparisons.

And the very fact that Chinese has had to depend on placement of its monosyllables to express all the relations for which speech is called upon, instead of relying on changes of form, seems to have, and indeed has so stimulated the development of pure linguistic power that the language is actually as perfect and clear a medium of cultured and learned intercourse, as is the Sanskrit, the supreme type of the so-called most developed form, the inflectional. And by reason of its possession of the ideographic element it has a vividness which the Sanskrit has not. No language can be a highly developed one which does not provide in some way for the expression of all possible needed relations between the three fundamental postulates of life and activity—the self, the action and the world; and Chinese does this in spite of its monosyllabic structure by the development of its syntax of position. And it should be remembered further that Chinese syntax, in strict correspondence to the genius of the language, is not the same formal thing that syntax is with our inflectional tongues, but includes, or rather is primarily based on the *harmonic adjustment of the inherent basic ideas of or within the words*. The Chinese monosyllables are then not the naked separate things they are in the dictionary, but the whole phrase or sentence is on the contrary as much a unit as one of ours; and often more so.

This integral unity of the whole sentence or expression, dominated by a perspective of ideas rather than of forms, which is achieved in Chinese by the elaboration of placement, is also characteristic of the structure of the languages of the American continent; but, these languages being polysyllabic, the vividness and unity are attained by a method described as Incorporation, whereby the accessories of relation are so included in or attached to the leading word that the whole expression assumes the form and sound of a single word. And a similar process takes place with the various elements of a compound sentence. So that although this one of the divisions of language approaches very closely to the Inflectional in its external forms, it yet has held to the vividness and essential characteristics of the ideographic method. And it is a point of the utmost importance for the decipherment of the Maya glyphs, to note as has been stated before, that their syntax of combination must follow that of the spoken language, which we know.

There is one broad line of division marking all the languages and civilizations of the world — the line between the ideographic and the literal; it marks the use of hieroglyphic or of alphabetic writing, and it denotes a culture so widely different from ours, modes of thought so distinct, views of life and man's relation to it one might almost say so opposite to ours, as to point unmistakably to a most distant past, and a former world-culture probably as wide-spread in its day as is now ours — or more so. And it is one of the strangest and most remarkable of the phenomena we are considering, that the two divisions have overlapped each other in time to such a degree that whereas we have in Sanskrit, the most perfect type of Aryan, or inflectional languages, the oldest of them all; on the other hand we have in Chinese an equally perfect linguistic medium of the other type, kept alive into our own times.

When we consider the development and status of the American civilizations which have been revealed to us, and especially when we have once opened our minds to the possibility that world-civilizations different in their time from ours in ours, may for all we know have existed and been blotted out ages ago, leaving linguistic traces, and perhaps perpetuating cultural remnants in a few parts of the earth, it is impossible not to recognize the breadth of the problem we are considering. All over the American continent at the time of the Discovery we see cultures and systems whose time had come. Back of most of the North and South American tribes we find the remains of mighty and utterly extinct civilizations — only their dim memory left. In the centers of higher culture from Mexico to Peru we see the ancient civilization brought further down to our own times; but there also, in process, all the incidents of break-up and an expiring greatness. Internecine strife, invasion from outside, changes of center, are all going on, and all marked by a *steady decrease* in everything that means civilization. Of the ancient mathematical and astronomical knowledge a corner of which is revealed to us by the Maya glyph remains, only a distorted fragment appears in the Mexican, where also hieroglyphs have yielded to a cruder rebus-writing. The stately and incomparable compositions and architecture of Palenque, Copan and Quiriguá have yielded to the ball courts and local strifes of Chichen Itza — all this following the very course of changing historical succession preserved in the Chronicles. The later the date, the lower in every case the culture; this is impossible not to recognize, nor have we traces of any different course of events. Of course we see the rise of the Aztec nation, a small cycle, but like the Gothic upon the Roman, it comes at the end of the general American break-up — an incursion of barbarians settling on and preserving for us fragments of the culture that preceded them, just as has happened over and over again all over the world. And the same with the Incas in Peru. And yet even the Mexican culture demands our high respect, comparing favorably with European of the same period. Indeed it was actually far ahead of the latter in matters of education and many points of polity.

But in spite of its seeming greatness, its heart and energy were gone, just as with Peru, and both yielded to what on the face seems a miracle, but was only the expression of that force which was preparing the American continent for a new race and civilization, still now only in its beginnings. The Mayan empire had already broken up. And even as we write, the archaeological history of the other hemisphere is being repeated here; on the heels of Manabi comes the Chimu Valley, and soon it will be with America as with Egypt—one will not be able to print an up-to-date work on its early history, for new discoveries will carry it back further, and to greater scope, before the previous ones can be edited and gotten to press. Compare the few pages of earliest Egypt in Sharpe's history, with Flinders Petrie's work of a decade or so ago, and that with the situation today.

It is a simple fact that decipherment and publication all over the world can no longer keep pace with discovery; and the time has come for archaeology to begin to survey these remnants, engineering works that would tax any modern nation with all our appliances, vast ruined cities, one above the other, innumerable languages and writings, the traces of peoples whose very names are lost to history—as a whole, and to ask itself how long it must have taken for all these works to be accomplished, let alone for the birth and decay of the civilizations that supported them, and gave environment for the development of such technical skill as could finish the enormous bulk of the Great Pyramid with an accuracy beyond the fineness of our best instruments to measure. For not only mere bulk is to be considered—though there is enough of that scattered over the earth to keep all the possible available craftsmen of the world a wholly incommensurate time achieving them, but the ability to conceive and carry out such works. What *sort* of people leveled Monte Alban for its crown of pyramids, dreamed and executed the stucco modelings of Palenque, built the temple of Boro Budur in Java, cut the Bamian statues of the Hindû Kush, and so on, and so on, for page after page? If they had such appliances as we have, they must be ranked at least in our class for having them; if they did them without our great engines, what sort of men were they? And if they could do these things without our appliances, is it not a fair inference that they could easily have made the tools, or others better perhaps?

One fact is becoming more prominent with every advance of archaeology over the world, a fact of the greatest linguistic interest, namely that ancient civilizations and empires, as a whole, *lasted longer* than ours of today. Consider how many different and successive empires Europe has had in the last 2000 odd years, *our* history; and how long each of our cultures has lasted. All of them put together would go into one of these older periods, and have plenty to spare. Passing over what may be the real meaning and bearing of this fact on the problem of universal history and human evolution, and the position of our race today, the linguistic considerations which follow are most interesting.

If the fundamental thesis of language as a human activity is its direct correspondence to and expression of all the inner motives and forces of the users, we have here a key to the survival to our day, an unknown period past its own time, of the Chinese type.

Of the development, modification and decay of languages we have ample material in our own times for study, the periods over which the modifying forces operate being an equal measure of the periods of national activity and change. And, what is perhaps not always sufficiently recognized, we have an elaboration of the formal elements going on under very different impulses, at different periods of the life of the language. The time has come in the history of a people for it to play a greater part on the world's stage: some danger has threatened the national life and aroused its energies, or other causes have worked to quicken the mental and spiritual life; an Elizabethan era is ushered in, frequently by a forerunner, a Chaucer, and the language responds, its forms develop and are perfected. Or else some fitting or amalgamating force comes in from outside, the life of the people is widened, new blood enters in every sense, and the forms of the language respond. Or perhaps, when they may seem to have come to the tether end of things, and men's minds turn back to older, even prehistoric times, seeds long buried and forgotten in the nature spring up, and a true national Renaissance follows. In these cases the change and elaboration of forms is a symptom of new life; the vehicle is being molded and expanded to fit the growing thought.

But it is not always so. There comes a time when the outgoing force, the activity of life, wanes and, after a greater or less period of settled conditions, a period of proper use and government of the regions occupied, a change sets in. And then we may have again the wholly deceptive phenomenon of linguistic amplification; but it is the false activity of decay. The energy has turned in and begun to feed upon itself. The national impulse has changed from achievement to gratification, more and more sources are drawn upon to minister to its enjoyment, and that enjoyment becomes an art; forms of every kind are subtly refined in its service, and linguistic forms with them. And this is then the very period when all these material, formal elements are pointed to with pride as the evidence of culture and progress. The thought-life of the nation has lost itself in the conflict and confusion, in the distractions of the forms into which it has molded the matter its creative force had entered.

We have thus in nations and languages, as in individuals, the phenomena of birth, growth, use, and a quick or a slow death, all marked by various degrees and signs of health or disease, and *every one at root a moral question*. These are the facts of general average, quite corresponding to those that form the bases for life insurance tables. But, as with these latter, not only are there variations for inheritance, class, locality, and so on, but there are here and there cases of out and out exception—which from all we can see must be assigned to some external force in operation on the individual. We call them "freak" occurrences, only because we cannot see the wider law or causes at work. When we meet them in sufficient numbers, we make new tables to cover them as far as we can, again in general only. Other causes still elude us, though they must have a fountain somewhere.

We have, as great exceptions to our general averages, two opposite phenomena. One is the sudden inexplicable and dazzling rise on the world's stage of a totally insignificant people, the other the seeming arrest for long periods of time of the normal processes of even incipient decay. And touching the latter point, it is strange indeed that in two such widely different cultures as those of Iceland and China we should find the same law apparently at work; the periods are vastly unlike in actual, but not so in relative duration. We have no way of properly placing the maintenance of Icelandic and Chinese as they have been other than by simply laying down the existence of what we may call a Law of Retardation, whose ultimate causes we cannot fathom or classify, but which will stand as an opposite phase of the Law of Stimulation, which is more frequent in operation, but is equally unexplained.

If we will now regard the languages and cultures of the world, we will find all the phases of linguistic and cultural activity, operative with about the same degree of rapidity, all over both hemispheres, save in places protected by our Law of Retardation. We will find the rate of changes and successions generally far less rapid the farther back in time we go; and finally we will find a special and marked acceleration on both sides of the Atlantic during the last thousand years, all incident to the placing of a new race in America.

So for the facts as we find them. They point to the descent of past American civilizations from a past period of continental, or far more probably, of world-wide extent. For who can imagine that people great enough to build as these did, should not also have navigated? Why should we assume in the face of other experiences, that Maya dates and calculations mean nothing, except on the general principle that they did not know as much as we do, and were doubtless liars? Bailly proved over a hundred years ago that Hindû exact astronomical observations must date back at least 5000 years, and that they were in possession of minutely accurate tables[20] long before Europe was. And the rotundity of the earth was certainly known both to them and the other great nations of antiquity.

Archaeology is today pushing back the dates of fixed and acknowledged history almost to the date given by the Egyptians to Solon for the submersion of the great Atlantean island; and if we can but read the Maya glyphs, and open *that* door, another twenty years from now may show us beyond all possible dispute evidences in every part of the earth belt of a contemporaneous culture, different from and precedent to the Aryan.

*   *   *   *   *

I have so far in this monograph, based upon and having to do as it has with the Maya glyphs, their interpretation and their place in the linguistic field, limited myself to an analysis and consideration of the facts presented to us by those linguistic and cultural data we have actually before us. But there is one further problem which is suggested by it all. It is this: Where, in point of time and place, is the change in the world's linguistic and cultural life from ideographic to literal to be sought for, and what is its rationale? Separated from us by such an enormous period of time as it is, I still cannot believe that some view of it cannot be had. There are various facts of Old World history and language, partly of prehistoric Europe, partly of Asia, an analysis of which would extend this paper too far into other fields; but apart entirely from the question of myths or traditions, there are various actual observed phenomena both of language and writing, especially in Central Asia, which do not fit into any of the ordinary theories, and which do

---

[20] *Traité de l'Astronomie Indienne et Orientale*, Disc. Prél. et seq.

suggest this, as a simple linguistic conclusion. In point of locality, at least, the conclusion agrees with the usual "Aryan home" theory; but as far as concerns this latter it must be remembered that however fully it demonstrates the unity of the Aryan race, beyond that fact all questions of dates and even of the state of civilization at the time, are not matters of history as yet for us, but only of theory — as to which our present "perspective" may be once more as faulty as it has often been heretofore.[21]

I believe that this center of transition lay somewhere in Central Asia, to the north of the great Himâlayan range. That this region was a sort of alembic, a melting-pot (as America is today) for various peoples of an ancient world-wide culture, as broad at least in its scope as the term Aryan is today. That this culture displayed the ideographic traits we have discussed, and that it has left more or less definite traces at different places in the world. That it covered the two Americas, in whatever continental form they may then have existed, leaving us there "les débris échappés à un naufrage commun." That coincident with a new and universal world-epoch, as wide in its cultural scope as the difference between the ideographic and literal, there was finally formed a totally new vehicle for the use of human thought, the inflectional, literal, alphabetic. That this vehicle was perfected into some great speech, the direct ancestor of Sanskrit, into the *forms* of which were concentrated all the old power of the ancient hieroglyphs and their underlying concepts. For Sanskrit, while the oldest is also the mightiest of Aryan grammars; and no one who has studied its forms, or heard its speech from educated native mouths, can call it anything but concentrated spiritual power. That the force which went on the one hand into the Sanskrit forms, was on the other perpetuated on into the special genius of Chinese, in which, as we know it, we have a retarded survival, not of course of outer form so much as of method and essence. And in Tibetan, in spite of all that is said to the contrary, I suspect that we have a derivative, not from either Chinese or Sanskrit as we know them, but by a medial line from a common point.[22] Of course the time for such changes must

[21] The suggestion above is linguistic, and in that phase is given as a corollary to the foregoing discussion; but, as stated, it is at the same time in accord with the "Aryan" theory in its essentials (though not in its hypothetical and ultra-historical speculations), and it also finds confirmation by various passages in *The Secret Doctrine*, by H. P. Blavatsky, as already quoted. "The traces of an immense civilization, even in Central Asia, are still to be found. This civilization is undeniably *prehistoric*.... The Eastern and Central portions of those regions — the Nan-Shan and the Altyn-Tagh — were once upon a time covered with cities that could well vie with Babylon. A whole geological period has swept over the land, since those cities breathed their last, as the mounds of shifting sand, and the sterile and now dead soil of the immense central plains of the basin of Tarim testify.... In the oasis of Cherchen some 300 human beings represent the relics of about a hundred extinct nations and races — the very names of which are now unknown to our ethnologists." (Vol. I, page xxxii et seq.) See also Col. Prjevalsky's *Travels*. Why should it not be so? The above was written in 1888, but the evidences are growing every day, and it will be against all archaeological precedent if far-reaching results do not follow from Dr. Stein's *small* find, and from Capt. d'Ollone's recent researches among the Lolos, and the securing by him, as we are informed, of the long-sought knowledge of their hieroglyphic system.

[22] The study of Tibetan has so far been approached almost exclusively from the south, that is by those already familiar with Sanskrit and Pâli. To this fact, as well as to the

have been enormous; but whatever it was, it was no greater in its realm as time, than were the mental differences in theirs. And they both are equally human data.

Certain other facts point to the American or Atlantic source and center of this ancient epoch. They are briefly that all around the Mediterranean basin we find traces of a vanished culture, unknown to our history, and living only in tradition and some archaeological remains. And of this culture various investigators, each approaching it from his particular favorite locality, have constructed for us as many different "Empires," by theories each supported by various details of analogies. One calls them Tartars, another Hittites, another Pelasgians, and so on. And all of them, in each of the theories, have as a fact a great many unexplained characteristics, different from those of our historical nations. Some of these characteristics, most markedly the Basque, but also not a few at greater distance, have definite American similarities. It might not be a far guess that these fragments represent an eastward movement, which later in the history of the Aryan development met and was pushed back westward again by the fully formed and dominant Aryan race from its Central Asian center. This is the future province of Archaeology.

And I am convinced that the widest door there is to be opened to this past of the human race, is that of the Maya glyphs. The narrow limitations of our mental horizon as to the greatness and dignity of man, of his past, and of human evolution, were set back widely by Egypt and what she has had to show, and again by the Sanskrit; but the walls are still there, and advances, however rapid, are but gradual. With the reading of America I believe the walls themselves will fall, and a new conception of past history will come.

---

overwhelming influence exercised on literary Tibetan by the Buddhist propaganda, is due the difficulty one meets in any study of its origins. The traces, however, do nevertheless exist. Some interesting facts concerning both Chinese and Tibetan, which seem to be entirely omitted in such later standard works as those of Summers, Wade, and Giles, are to be found in the almost forgotten *Chinese Grammar* of Dr. Marshman, Serampore, 1814.

Lector House believes that a society develops through a two-fold approach of continuous learning and adaptation, which is derived from the study of classic literary works spread across the historic timeline of literature records. Therefore, we aim at reviving, repairing and redeveloping all those inaccessible or damaged but historically as well as culturally important literature across subjects so that the future generations may have an opportunity to study and learn from past works to embark upon a journey of creating a better future.

This book is a result of an effort made by Lector House towards making a contribution to the preservation and repair of original ancient works which might hold historical significance to the approach of continuous learning across subjects.

HAPPY READING & LEARNING!

LECTOR HOUSE LLP
E-MAIL: lectorpublishing@gmail.com